SEEING OUR WORLD THROUGH DIFFERENT EYES

SEEING OUR WORLD THROUGH DIFFERENT EYES

Thoughts on Space and Time, Abraham Lincoln, and God

Markolf H. Niemz, PhD

Translated by James David Dunn

WIPF & STOCK · Eugene, Oregon

SEEING OUR WORLD THROUGH DIFFERENT EYES
Thoughts on Space and Time, Abraham Lincoln, and God

Copyright © 2020 Markolf H. Niemz. All rights reserved. Except for brief quotations in critical publications or reviews, no part of this book may be reproduced in any manner without prior written permission from the publisher. Write: Permissions, Wipf and Stock Publishers, 199 W. 8th Ave., Suite 3, Eugene, OR 97401.

Wipf & Stock
An Imprint of Wipf and Stock Publishers
199 W. 8th Ave., Suite 3
Eugene, OR 97401

www.wipfandstock.com

PAPERBACK ISBN: 978-1-7252-8545-3
HARDCOVER ISBN: 978-1-7252-8546-0
EBOOK ISBN: 978-1-7252-8547-7

Manufactured in the U.S.A.

Contents

Comments by James David Dunn 9
How to Get Clues 13

First Challenge: Space and Time 19
Which Comes First—Space or Time? 20
Newton's Ships 21
Clarke's Bucket 23
Kant's Intuitions 25
Space and Time Are Not Two 27

Second Challenge: Being and Becoming 41
Which Comes First—Being or Becoming? 42
Parmenides' Sphere 43
Heraclitus' Fire 45
Light's Memory 47
Being and Becoming Are Not Two 55

Third Challenge: Good and Evil 65
Which Comes First—Good or Evil? 66
Leibniz' Theodicy 67
Laplace's Demon 71
Libet's Experiment 74
Good and Evil Are Not Two 81

Fourth Challenge: Chicken and Egg — 89
    Which Comes First—the Chicken or the Egg? — 90
    Cuvier's Fossils — 92
    Lamarck's Giraffes — 93
    Darwin's Tree of Life — 95
    Chicken and Egg Are Not Two — 103

Fifth Challenge: Creator and Creation — 111
    Which Comes First—Creator or Creation? — 112
    Moses' Genesis — 115
    Hawking's Universe — 118
    Whitehead's Organism — 120
    Creator and Creation Are Not Two — 132

Sixth Challenge: Love and Understanding — 137
    Which Comes First—Love or Understanding? — 138
    True Love — 143
    True Understanding — 148
    True Happiness — 155
    Love and Understanding Are Not Two — 160

Bonus Chapter — 166
    Einstein's Relativity and Near-Death Experiences — 167

Talk with the Author — 177
Definitions Used in This Book — 182
Lucy's Children Foundation — 185
Notes — 190
Picture Credits — 198
Contact the Author — 200

to us all

**A COSMOS
IN WHICH LIFE JUST HAPPENS
IS AS CREATIVE AS ANY GOD CAN BE.**

Comments by James David Dunn

It's not every day that an award-winning biophysicist will invite you to translate his work into English. And this is all the more surprising because Professor Niemz knows his English just as well as I do. But I believe that he had much more in mind. Yes, we translated the book into American English in the clearest of terms possible, prepared especially for inquiring minds of English-speaking people in our modern culture. And there is no doubt that his message and contribution to society will open the minds and perspectives for humankind for many more years to come.

But what did Professor Niemz really have in mind? To make a difference! He wishes to inspire *me*, the translator, and *you*, the reader, to view all of us together as citizens of a living cosmos, a living world who breathes our same breath and lives our experiences—experiences that are felt deeply by a loving nature with unifying power and visions of the future that move our very experience and destiny.

Something creates our world directly, continuously and eternally as a fully-determined, organic and evolving system that is permeated and actuated by a single power. And this "something" holds the deepest secret of life and the final consolation and joy of all creation.

Constantly regard the universe as one living being, having one substance and one soul; and observe how all things have reference to one perception, the perception of this one living being; and how all things act with one movement; and how all things are the cooperating causes of all things which exist.[A1]

But for now, humanity has taken the wrong turn. If we don't correct it, our species will be rubbed out and replaced. Only if we follow nature and embrace all living things—not our obsessive egos—can we get in sync again with an infinite mind and world that loves us all.

Professor Niemz gives us clues to discover the perspective that we've lost. During quiet moments of desperation, we might ask ourselves: Who are we? Why are we here? Where are we going? What happens when we die? We enter upon a quest for truth, and he is our guide. We question the origin of our existence, space-time, good-evil, chicken-egg, creator-creation, and discover the one underlying truth that moves our world and even the most insignificant particle in the cosmos.

At this very moment, we are all co-authoring our lives with our world that feels and experiences every impulse: All living energy is transmitted at the speed of light and stored in the mind of the cosmos—all thoughts and experiences. Every heartbeat is a tropism changing the face of the world in transcendent progression and synchrony. It breathes with us, we breathe with it. We are all connected: Whatever we do to others, we do to ourselves. At death, the light from each moment of our life joins with the canvas of stars.

Throughout our translations and during many conversations between me and Professor Niemz, one thing became clear: There is an eternal play of destiny that compels every living thing during the pulse of each moment—an unending momentum of intelligence that links us with a continuum of all living phenomena. Whether we like it or not, we are all players in a transcendent drama in which this intelligence—

or God—might not even know how things will work out. And into this very second, we continue as part of its living *dramatis personae*. God is our being lived in its reality as one. Beyond all of space-time and good-evil, everything becomes known. All living things embrace their final synthesis of joy. Yes, we are cosmic apocalypse in our own making. We contribute to a never-ending story. Never assume that Einstein's famous theory of relativity doesn't have divine implications. There is not only a theory of relativity of space and time, but also a theory of *living* relativity and connectedness.

Light sees the span of our lifetime in less than a heartbeat from the other side of eternity. Please consider the final thought from *The Bridge of San Luis Rey* by Thornton Wilder: "Soon we will die." We ourselves will be loved for a while and forgotten. But the love will have been enough. All those impulses of love return to the love that made them. Even memory is not necessary for love. There is a land of the living and a land of the dead, and the bridge is love, the only survival, the only meaning.

> Do you fall down, you millions?
> Do you sense your creator, world?
> Seek him beyond the canopy of stars . . .[A2]
> *Everything is truly one thing.*[A3]

I am personally indebted to Markolf for his kindness, sensitivity and example as a remarkable human being and teacher. During this work, he has become my friend and brother: We are all children with the cosmos.

—James David Dunn
South Padre Island, USA

How to Get Clues

> WHEN YOU WISH TO FIND A CLUE,
> TRY TO CHANGE YOUR POINT OF VIEW!

Which came first—**the chicken or the egg?** I am pretty sure that you have already tried to unlock this challenging riddle. I was still a teenager when I came across it for the very first time. Back then I felt—as most people do—that there can't be a logical answer to this puzzle. If the chicken came first, where did this very first chicken originally come from? And if the egg came first, who had originally laid this very first egg? From a purely logical point of view, there doesn't seem to be any way out of this vicious circle.

But there is a unique solution, and in this book we will learn what it is. Once you understand how the riddle works, the solution is straightforward; and it can help us discover who we really are in the universe. Our solution even has the power to unlock the riddle to find (no kidding) God! This is because we can transform our original riddle to something far greater: Which came first—**creator or creation?** For pious readers, the answer is clear: "The creator, of course!" Others will oppose: "There is no creator. How could there be a creation?" Soon we will realize that there is a much deeper and all-embracing solution than these two. But what could it be? Did I get your attention? You must now be very hungry to get straight into this book, and that's what an introduction is all about. Pretty good for just one page, right?

How to Get Clues

As we get started, I would like to share something very important with you: the true secret of *how to get clues*. Let's assume you spend your holidays in Yosemite National Park taking photographs of its breathtaking landscape. Suddenly you notice a bird's tail peeking out behind some big rocks as shown in figure 1 left. But what bird is it? You can't tell from this one picture! But if you now change your point of view *in space* by taking a second picture from a few steps to your left, you can easily tell that this bird must be a Steller's Jay (figure 1 right).

Fig. 1: Which bird is peeking out behind these rocks?

Ready for another lucid example? So let's now assume you spend your next holidays in Italy taking photographs of the sea. You're so impressed that you forget what time it is. All you can see is the scenery shown in figure 2 left. So you might ask yourself: Is this a sunrise or a sunset? Is it morning or evening? You can't tell from this one glimpse! But if you now change your point of view *in time* by taking a second picture a few moments later, you can easily tell from the rising sun that it must be morning (figure 2 right).

How to Get Clues

Fig. 2: Is this a sunrise or a sunset?

You might argue that there can't be any secret to these examples because we all know how to look behind a rock and how to make out a sunrise from a sunset. Sure, I agree. Yet there is a common strategy pursued in these two examples that discloses the secret about how to get clues: When you wish to find a clue, try to change your point of view! That is, we need to view things from several perspectives to better understand. In the six challenges ahead, we will apply this strategy not only to space and time, but also to our fellow man and to nature herself. We will learn that no human being is born to be a culprit and that there is a divine justice out there surpassing all human imagination.

With this being said, I am now going to outline some upcoming highlights for you. Our journey kicks off with a puzzle that is related to the fundamental structures of our world: Which comes first—**space or time?** Join us when we listen to Sir Isaac Newton and Immanuel Kant doing philosophy on space and time. They both strongly influenced our way of thinking, but it wasn't until 1905 that a twenty-six-year-old physicist solved the puzzle: Albert Einstein.

In the second challenge, we will apply the same type of question to two other features of our world: Which comes first—**being or becoming?** Is the universe about *being* something or about *becoming* something? This problem stumped Greek philosophers already 2,500 years ago. We'll learn that there are countless realities and also something very special that truly deserves the name "eternity."

Now that you've got the knack of this book, we'll keep it going: Which comes first—**good or evil?** It was Gottfried Wilhelm Leibniz who once declared that we live in the best of all possible worlds. But Pierre-Simon Laplace argued that a predestined world isn't given any chance to become better. Does nature provide any freedom? And if she does, how do "good" and "evil" come about?

Have you ever heard of Cuvier's fossils or of Lamarck's giraffes? Make sure that you don't miss out our challenge 4! Both Cuvier and Lamarck paved the way for Charles Darwin's theory of evolution that helps us solve the mother of all mysteries: Which comes first—**the chicken or the egg?** Upon discussing the solution, we will reveal a great inconsistency: Most of us agree with Darwin that no species was created individually—so why do we still believe in every human being's individuality?

And then it'll be your turn: Which comes first—**creator or creation?** This puzzle is probably one of the deepest ever. Just give it a try and apply all that you have learned so far! I can tell you that this puzzle has very much in common with "chicken or egg." We'll plunge directly into Moses' Genesis and into Stephen Hawking's universe. I will also introduce you to one of the *finest* philosophers I've come across: Alfred

North Whitehead. Most of us haven't even heard his name, yet he's the one who holds the most vital solution of all for us. Whitehead teaches us how to love a God that truly is a God of every living thing.

The final chapter reflects the relationship between our main sources of truth—religion and science. It's remarkable to see how much humanity has been able to profit from both of them equally for so many centuries. The symmetry of a honeycomb or a snowflake inspires just as many religious feelings as a prayer. Here, we'll get right down to it: Which comes first—**love or understanding?**

In the bonus chapter, I'm going to disclose four clues to you that truly changed my life. All these clues link spiritual experiences to Einstein's famous theory of relativity. I admit that I still have goosebumps when I think about what these clues really mean altogether: *There's "something" around us and everywhere in outer space that guarantees the laws of nature and keeps track of every single move that we make.*

I am happy that you have taken notice of my book. It is up to you to decide how you will use the messages that you are going to read. I do not intend to bring you around to my line of thinking or to change your views in any way. I want precisely the opposite thing from you: I expect you to question and scrutinize every thought that you will read. Only in this way will it be possible for a world view to develop that is whole and in unity with everything that we know about life and the cosmos.

—Markolf H. Niemz

First Challenge: Space and Time

First Challenge: Space and Time

Which Comes First—Space or Time?

> LIKE A COIN THEY CHANGE THEIR FACE:
> SPACE TO TIME, AND TIME TO SPACE.

There are two "basic structures" in our world that we all are aware of, but it seems that no one can really tell what they are: space and time. Have you ever asked yourself: What is this immaterial skeleton that we call *space*? And what is this irreversible beat that we call *time*? I have absorbed how our smartest philosophers conceived space and time—yet there is just one definition that fits today's world of science. It was Albert Einstein who came up with this definition when he was asked about the nature of time: **"Time" is what I read off my watch.**[1] (I will highlight all major definitions in blue color.) Now let me complete Einstein's definition: **... and "space" is what I read off my ruler.** Both definitions, trivial as they might seem, include one of the most famous theories of modern science: the theory of relativity. You can feel the relativity shining through once you stress the words "I" and "my" in both of these definitions.

Which comes first—space or time? In order to answer this question, we need to know how space and time *relate* to one another. Is space superior to time, or is time superior to space? Can there be space without time, or can there be time without space? Have you ever thought about this? I can tell you that our smartest philosophers have, but they came up with different answers. Until 1905, space and time were considered two fundamental structures of the universe that are also independent of each other. So, there were good reasons to believe that space could exist without time—and that time could exist without space. But, when diving into space and time, we must not be surprised. Our conception of the world may end up inside out.

Newton's Ships

Talking about space and time, we have to begin somewhere in history. Let's begin with someone special who still has a deep impact on how we conceive our world today: Sir Isaac Newton, English mathematician, physicist, and theologian. In his own day, when people didn't yet distinguish between science and theology, Newton was a "natural philosopher."

Sir Isaac Newton,
English polymath
(1642 – 1726/27)

At the age of forty-four, he published his famous work *Philosophiae Naturalis Principia Mathematica*. In this book, he considers both time and space *absolute*. **Something is "absolute" if it does not depend on the observer's perspective.** Newton writes: "Absolute, true and mathematical time, of itself, and from its own nature flows equably without regard to anything external."[2] And in the following paragraph, he informs us about space: "Absolute space, in its own nature, without regard to anything external, remains always similar and immovable."[3]

Let's make out how Newton arrived at these properties of time and space. With respect to time, he explains: "Absolute time, in astronomy, is distinguished from relative, by the equation or correction of the vulgar time. For the natural days are truly unequal, though they are commonly considered as equal, and used for a measure of time; astronomers correct this inequality for their more accurate deducing of the celestial motions."[4] So, what Newton does here is basic science—observing! He is observing that astronomy is more accurate when assuming an absolute time. Unfortunately for him, time may not be any object to observe.

With respect to space, Newton observed **ships** moving under sail:[5] He defines *relative location* of a body as that part of a ship which the body possesses; this part moves together with the ship. Next, he defines *relative motion* of a body as its translation from one location inside the ship into another. And then, he defines *absolute rest* as "the continuance of the body in the same part of that immovable space in which the ship itself, its cavity, and all that it contains, is moved."[6] So, Newton is not really deriving absolute space. He's speaking of "relative location" and "relative motion," and eventually the term "immovable space" pops up.

As we will learn soon, Newton was mistaken regarding his views of absolute space and absolute time; but this does not in any way lessen his great contributions to mechanics. The so-called *Newton's laws of motion* are three physical laws that, put together, are the foundation of classical mechanics. We still learn them in school today. These laws describe the relationship between a body, the forces acting upon it, and its motion in response to these forces.

Clarke's Bucket

Newton's thoughts sparked a lot of academic interest at that time. German polymath Gottfried Wilhelm Leibniz was one of his strongest opponents. But Newton didn't oppose Leibniz personally. It was Samuel Clarke, Newton's spokesman, who fought the battle against Leibniz to defend Newton's conception of absolute space and time.

Samuel Clarke,
English philosopher
(1675 – 1729)

Leibniz argued that space can't be absolute because it would contradict what he termed "the principle of sufficient reason."[7] Here is his argument: If there were absolute space, then the universe would have been created at some particular location in that absolute space; but there is no sufficient reason why it should have this particular location. So, Leibniz actually makes use of symmetry: Space can't be absolute because no location in space is distinct from the others.

Clarke hit back with his **bucket** argument:[8] Water in a bucket, hung from a rope and set to rotate, will start with a flat surface (figure 3 left). As the water begins to spin in the bucket, it is accelerated and the surface of the water becomes concave (figure 3 center). If the bucket is stopped, the water continues to spin, and while the spin continues, the surface of the water remains concave (figure 3 right). But since the surface is concave regardless of whether the bucket is spinning or not, Clarke argued: There must be some other thing outside of the bucket—absolute space in which the water is accelerated; it can't accelerate with regard to nothing.

Fig. 3: Clarke's bucket argument

The point Clarke is making is that space must be absolute because movement can only be observed in relation to something else. But Clarke neglects the observable fact that there's always another object in space serving as a reference point with respect to moving; by doing so, he also neglects earth's gravity. The only "thing" that couldn't move against anything else would be space itself.

We could reflect more on both Clarke and Leibniz, but it would lead to a dead end. So let's go on instead and see how Kant at first tried and how Einstein finally succeeded in turning Clarke's bucket inside out.

Kant's Intuitions

It's the year 1770 when German philosopher Immanuel Kant submitted his script *Forms and Principles of the Sensible and Intelligible Worlds*. In this legendary PhD thesis, Kant writes: "Space is not something objective and real, nor a substance, nor an accident, nor a relation; instead, it is subjective and ideal, and originates from the mind's nature in accord with a stable law as a scheme."[9]

Immanuel Kant,
German philosopher
(1724 – 1804)

Kant's writings aren't that easy to read and understand. So let me try to play back his words in plain language. Kant is saying that space isn't part of reality; space doesn't exist anywhere but in our brains (figure 4 left). With such an odd conception of space, of course, Kant upset most scientists at that time who followed Newton in viewing space as a coordinate system inherent to nature herself (figure 5 left).

First Challenge: Space and Time

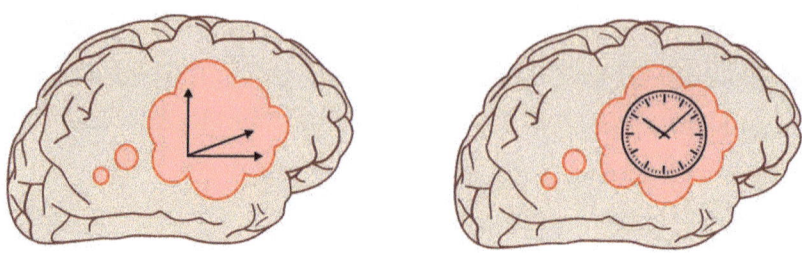

Fig. 4: Space and time according to Kant

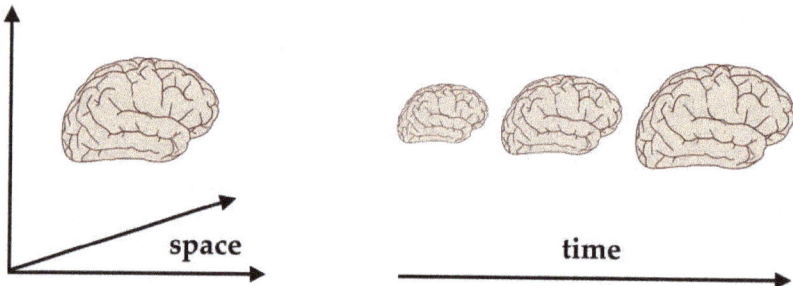

Fig. 5: Space and time according to Newton

But Immanuel Kant didn't give in. In the year 1789, he put even more wood on the fire with his famous *Critique of Pure Reason:* He claimed space to be an *"a priori* **intuition,"**[10] meaning that it is based on an *assumed* principle rather than on *observed* facts. Please recall that Newton and Clarke had tried to derive space from observing! Kant's argument is just one sentence long: "We can never represent to ourselves the absence of space, but we can quite well think it as empty of objects."[11] In other words: Space has to be a product of our brains because we can think of it only as an entity to contain something or not, but we can't grasp the idea of "there is no space" as we can with observable objects.

Regarding time, Immanuel Kant jumps to similar conclusions: Time, too, is an *"a priori* **intuition**"[12] since we can't imagine the absence of time, but we can surely think of time void of phenomena.[13] So, even time exists only in our brains (figure 4 right) and not outside of them as Isaac Newton had claimed (figure 5 right). Yet these brains in themselves show that Kant is wrong: Brains are getting older, and this process of aging is an *observable* fact since it is very easy to measure the decreasing activity of cells in time.

So we must be aware of pitfalls in Kant's philosophy. If his ideas were right, then our brains would provide us with space and time to experience reality. That is: Space and time would merely be a framework set up by our brains. Nevertheless, Kant deserves credit for having conceived space and time as being related to ourselves.

In 1905, Albert Einstein—a physicist and patent agent living in Switzerland—took up Kant's idea of space and time being subjective. Einstein unlocked them from our brains and published a new theory that was to revolutionize our conception of space and time.

Space and Time Are Not Two

Albert Einstein is famous for his theory of relativity—a work of formulas. But don't worry: The basic idea of this amazing theory can also be communicated in subtle images. So now I cordially invite you to something truly special. Welcome to Einstein's spacetime!

27

First Challenge: Space and Time

Einstein assumed only two things:[14] The speed of light is a natural constant (a number that never changes its value); the laws of nature have the same mathematical form for all "non-accelerating"[15] observers. From these two assumptions alone, he concluded that both time and space must be *relative*. **Something is "relative" if it depends on the observer's perspective.** Temporal ("timelike") and spatial ("spacelike") distances also depend on how fast an object or a process is moving relative to me. For example, when a watch moves relative to me, it is going slower from my perspective than a watch that I am wearing on my arm—even if both watches are identical!

Let's think out loud and visualize why time behaves so strangely: Figure 6 shows a cart at rest that is carrying a so-called *light clock*. The light clock is made up of only two mirrors and a particle of light, which is reflected back and forth between them. The light particle is colored yellow, its path of motion green. Each time the light particle bounces on the lower mirror, the clock "ticks" and one unit of time (like a second) has elapsed.

Fig. 6: Light clock in a cart at rest

When the cart is moving as in figure 7, the light particle travels along the dotted (longer!) path during two "ticks." With Einstein's assumption of a constant speed of light, we see that more time elapses between two consecutive "ticks" in figure 7 than between two consecutive "ticks" in figure 6. So, clocks go slower from my perspective if they move relative to me. This effect is called *time dilation* in Einstein's theory of relativity, but it is perceived only at very high speeds close to the speed of light.

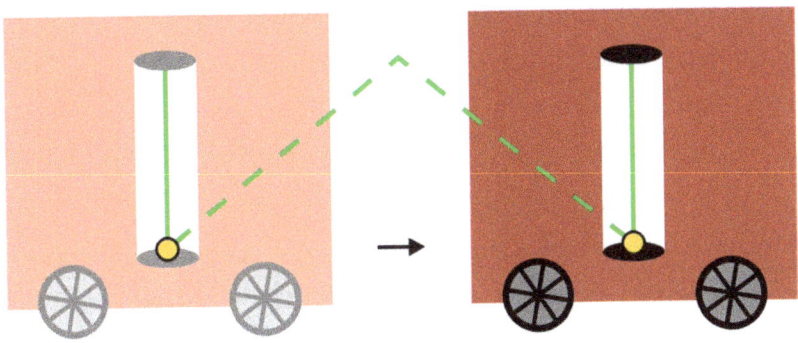

Fig. 7: Light clock in a moving cart

So, time isn't necessarily the same for all observers: It is relative and not absolute; universal time is an illusion. Even the atomic clock inside the *National Institute of Standards and Technology* in Boulder, Colorado, goes slower from my perspective when I move relative to it! Only temporal *distances* are real although their numeric values vary from observer to observer. So we're well-advised to not conceive "time" as a noun, but always as an adjective: "temporal" or "timelike." Time is not set in stone.

First Challenge: Space and Time

Many of the things that we have just experienced about temporal distances apply 1:1 to spatial distances too. Both are so closely linked with each other in Einstein's theory of relativity that we really must not view them separately. The very same distance appearing temporal to one observer can be spatial to a different observer if both observers move at very high speed relative to each other ("very high" meaning very close to the speed of light). This thought implies that not only absolute time is an illusion, but also absolute space (space being the same for all observers). For example, when a ruler moves relative to me, it is shorter from my perspective than a ruler that I am holding in my hand—even if both rulers are identical!

Let's think out loud a bit more so that we can understand why space behaves so strangely too: Figure 8 shows a stopwatch that is moving at almost the speed of light along a very long ruler at rest. From the ruler's perspective, this process might take a total of 15 seconds to go from one end of the ruler to the other. But the stopwatch shows only ten seconds because it is moving relative to the ruler and is thus going slower—as we have seen earlier.

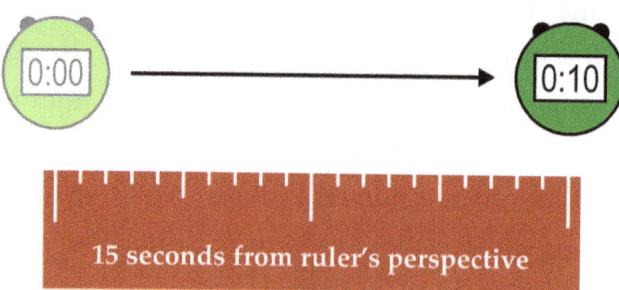

Fig. 8: Stopwatch is moving along a ruler at rest

Figure 9 illustrates the very same process, but from the stopwatch's perspective: Here, the ruler is moving along the stopwatch. From the stopwatch's perspective, the ruler must be shorter because it gets completely past the stopwatch in just ten seconds. Please recall that from the ruler's perspective (shown in figure 8), the same process takes 15 seconds. So, rulers are shorter from my perspective if they move relative to me. This effect is called *length contraction* in Einstein's theory of relativity, but—again—it is perceived only at very high speeds close to the speed of light.

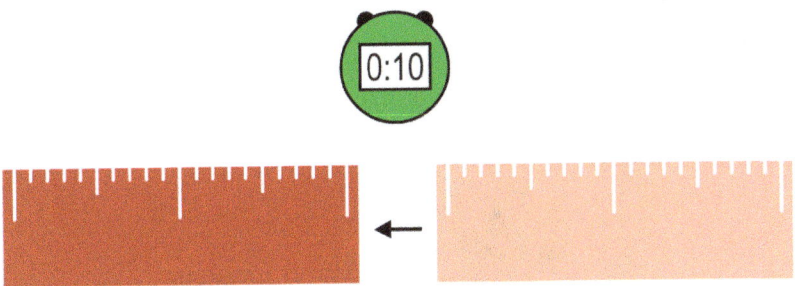

Fig. 9: Ruler is moving along a stopwatch at rest

So, space isn't necessarily the same for all observers either: Also, space is relative and not absolute; universal space is an illusion. Even the *International Prototype Meter* in Paris, France, is shorter from my perspective when I move relative to it! Only spatial *distances* are real although their numerical values vary from observer to observer. So we're also well-advised to not conceive "space" as a noun, but always as an adjective: "spatial" or "spacelike." Space is not set in stone either.

What I just outlined here is Einstein's *Special Theory of Relativity*.[16] It describes the relativity of spatial and temporal distances, but it doesn't yet take into account the influence of mass and energy. In the year 1915, Einstein put all of this together and published the *General Theory of Relativity*.[17] He was able to show that spatial and temporal distances do not only depend on the observer's perspective, but also on the presence of any surrounding mass and energy. For example, the sun's gravity deflects the light from stars. The same star at some location A seen by an observer on the sun appears at location B to an observer on the earth (figure 10). During a total solar eclipse in the year 1919, Einstein's prediction was clearly confirmed.[18]

Albert Einstein,
German-born physicist
(1879 – 1955)

Temporal distances, too, are altered by mass and energy: A clock goes more slowly the closer it is to the center of our planet because it is exposed to a greater force of gravity. If two identical clocks on a huge church tower are separated by 300 feet, the lower clock will lose one hour in ten billion years compared with the higher clock (figure 11). So that's why inhabitants living on a lower level in a high-rise complex will age a bit more slowly than inhabitants on an upper level. But the effect is so small that we won't notice it.

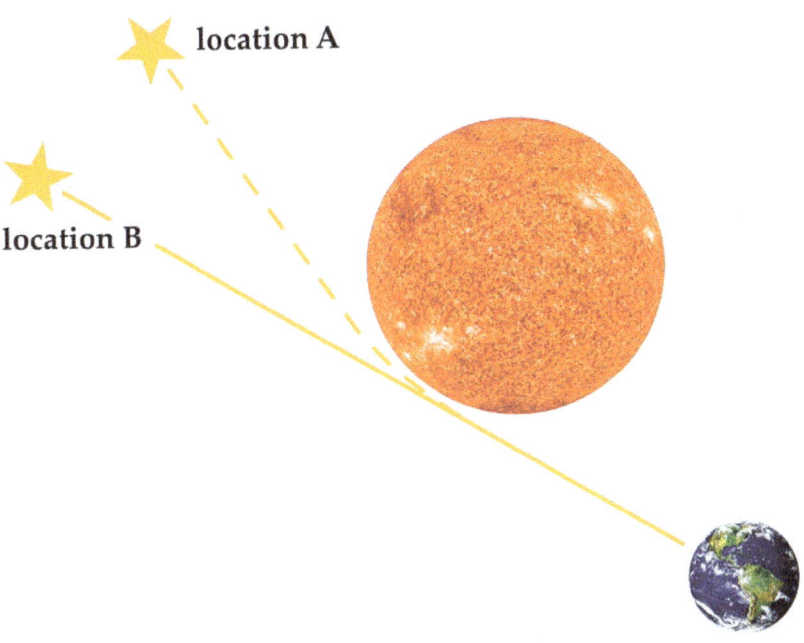

Fig. 10: Influence of gravity on spatial distances (not to scale)

Fig. 11: Influence of gravity on temporal distances

First Challenge: Space and Time

To this day, no one has been able to disprove Einstein's theory of relativity. That's why most physicists believe in it. Einstein's theory comes with a very persuasive argument: A *four-dimensional spacetime* can be constructed mathematically from space and time, which has the great advantage of distances in spacetime being absolute. Space and time *alone* are not fundamental to nature, but emerge from a deeper level of truth. So, our first challenge is likewise the biggest that physics is facing today—most of us still believe in space and time as if either of them existed alone.

There is more: That part of a distance that we perceive as spatial (or temporal) depends on our own state of motion and on the presence of mass and energy around us. That is: The very same distance can be *spatially* experienced by me, but *temporally* experienced by you! What's going on here? Well, we already discussed an example that illustrates this remarkable phenomenon: When a watch moves at very high speed relative to me, it is going slower from my perspective than my own watch. In other words: From my perspective, the other watch is completing less temporal distance than I am, but—at the same time—it's completing a great spatial distance because it's moving at very high speed relative to me. From its own perspective, the other watch is only completing temporal distance (it's aging), but no spatial distance (it isn't moving at all relative to itself).

These ideas lead us to a very interesting interpretation of Einstein's spacetime: It forms the framework for all things *to become*. Yet this general kind of "becoming" is not limited to time, instead it takes place both temporally *and* spatially: In spacetime, everything completes temporal and/or spatial distances. We experience temporal becoming as "moving in time" (aging) and spatial becoming as "moving in space." From my perspective, there are two extreme types of becoming: *I myself* am always completing temporal distances only (I am aging), but no spatial distance (I am not moving at all relative to myself); *light* is moving so fast that it is completing spatial distances only, but no temporal distance. So, light is never aging!

Einstein quickly conceived that the theory of relativity has a very deep impact on our conception of space and time: "People had believed that if everything disappears from the world, only space and time will remain; but according to the theory of relativity, space and time would disappear along with everything as well."[19] This is, indeed, how physicists view space and time today: Space and time don't exist without any mass or energy because they actually are qualities of mass and energy. We could also say that space and time are adjectives like "small" or "red." They're tangible in just that way; and they are highly variable as they're not the same for all observers. In figure 12, I tried to illustrate space and time as adjectives. Just compare it with figures 4 and 5, and you'll get an idea of how revolutionary Einstein's approach was.

Fig. 12: Space and time according to Einstein

First Challenge: Space and Time

> Please note: Only for a better readability, we'll still be speaking of "space" and "time"; but whenever we do so, we have the adjectives "spatial" and "temporal" in our minds.

And now this is really getting exciting: Since space and time are adjectives and not nouns, it doesn't make sense to ask about a beginning or an end of space and time. A noun like a table, of course, has a beginning and an end—when it's made and when it's decomposed. But please, could there be any beginning or end of "small" and "red"?

We physicists are now and then asked when and where our universe actually began to exist. According to the standard model of astrophysics, the universe is supposed to have started from a gigantic big bang some 14 billion years ago.[20] Keep in mind that even this value depends on the observer's perspective! Space and time originated from a primal point: a so-called *singularity*. All energy had been concentrated in this hot point and was later transformed to matter because of expansion and cooling. In the year 1931, Belgian physicist and theologian George Lemaître was the first to describe an expanding universe.[21] The term "big bang" was coined later by British astrophysicist Sir Fred Hoyle.[22] Hoyle was never convinced of a big bang—even until his death. He liked to refer to "big bang" to illustrate the biggest fallacy of the idea of a dynamic universe: What could have made a "big bang" at a time when matter didn't even exist? Nothing! There can only be noise in a material medium like air.

The hazy term "bang" is covering up our own lack of knowledge. Even so, many physicists believe in the big bang theory because it is best in fitting the great amount of data gathered by telescopes searching the cosmos. For example, big bang theory is consistent with our observations that all galaxies are moving away from each other and that the cosmos is radiating almost uniformly from every direction. In the year 1992, the satellite COBE measured the temperature distribution of cosmic background radiation and sent all of this data to earth. In figure 13, the temperature distribution is projected onto a plane, similar to a map of the earth: All the red areas are somewhat warmer than the blue areas, but the temperature variations never exceed .0001 percent.[23]

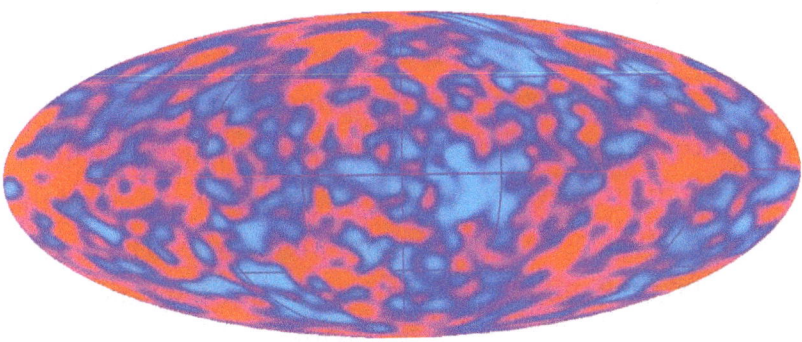

Fig. 13: Cosmic background radiation

So, indeed, the universe might have been concentrated within a hot point many years ago. Whether it was 14 billion years ago remains to be seen. This number has been adjusted upward by 8 billion years in just 50 years![24] However, I consider the hypothesis that space and time came into being with the big bang to be logically false. Three reasons come to my mind. I already mentioned the first one: Adjectives don't "pop up." Second, the attempt to equate the origin of space and time with the origin of energy (the bearer of these qualities) fails since all cosmic energy is and will always remain constant according to the law of the conservation of energy. Even energy has neither a beginning nor an end; energy can only be converted from one form (for example, solar energy) to another (for example, electricity). It always makes my hair stand on end when I hear politicians talking of "alternative sources of energy." There is no source of energy.

The third reason comes to us with a bit of logic: Space and time can't come into being because they would have to presume themselves to exist before they come into being in the first place. Every creation (including a creation of space or time) is a "becoming," and becoming is only possible in space and time. Hence, space and time require the previous existence of themselves to be created. If they started with the big bang, they were already there before the bang—and that is impossible. So we're going around in circles. The birth of space and time can't be hidden away in any big bang theory simply because it was never possible.

Also, space and time can never disappear: They would have disappeared only if "somewhere" and "somewhen" space and time didn't exist anymore. But there is no "somewhere" without space, and there is no "somewhen" without time. So we have even more circles! There is only one solution to get rid of all the circles: Space and time have no beginning and no end.

If I blew your mind with my thoughts on spacetime, I must apologize. To make up for everything, I'd like to give you a piece of advice along the way. In the future, always view time as temporal distance: some number that has been given a unit of time (for example "second"). Kindly note: It's a number that you read off your watch! Numbers can be as great or as small as you would like. You will never reach the end of all positive numbers or of all negative numbers; and you already understand why there can't be a beginning nor an end of time. Guess what? The same is true for space and spatial distances—assuming that you give your numbers a unit of length (for example "feet"). It's also a number that you read off your ruler! And now it must be instantly clear to you why space is boundless.

So, which comes first—space or time? Since numbers have no beginning and no end, the answer is very obvious: Neither one comes first. Space and time have always been there, and neither one of both qualities can exist alone. There is no space without time, and no time without space.

We will finish each of our challenges with a short summary:

> Message of our first challenge:
> *There is no space without time,*
> *and no time without space.*
>
> Alternative ways to express this message:
> *Space and time are not two.*
> *Space and time are two sides of the same coin.*
>
> The coin's name is: *distance.*

Second Challenge: Being and Becoming

Second Challenge: Being and Becoming

Which Comes First—Being or Becoming?

> WHAT WE DO RIGHT NOW AND HERE,
> EVER SHINES IN HEAVEN'S SPHERE.

What would you say if someone told you that he's watching Abraham Lincoln *live* serving as 16th president of the United States? No way! Right? But you're in for quite a surprise as you'll see in our second challenge. We will discuss powerful examples that will help us understand how incomplete our view of reality is. **"Reality" is how I perceive the world in space and time.** There isn't just one reality in the universe; instead, every observer in the universe has his/her/its reality depending on how the absolute distances in spacetime split into spatial and temporal. Please recall that space and time are relative, so how could there be one reality for all?

Philosophers frequently consider space the playground of being, and time the playground of becoming. Just think about it: How could I ever *be* if there were no such thing as space? How could I ever *become* if there were no such thing as time? It makes sense, right? Yet I'm afraid it isn't as easy as it sounds. Do you consider yourself a "human being"? Of course, you do! I did so myself until I started composing this challenge. But has it ever occurred to you that you might be a "human becoming" instead? It's not only your body aging; it's also your feelings, your knowledge, and your thoughts that *become* richer with every experience that you have. So what's our world all about—being or becoming?

Parmenides' Sphere

Parmenides of Elea was a Greek philosopher who was one of the first to scrutinize the nature of being and becoming. Let's turn back time 2,500 years and listen to his words: "It is impossible for anything not to be. If it came from nothing, what need could have made it arise later rather than sooner? If it came into being, it is not; nor is it if it is going to be in the future. Thus is becoming extinguished."[25]

Parmenides,
Greek philosopher
(sixth/fifth century BC)

From a logical point of view, Parmenides is a bit hasty in extinguishing any becoming. To truly understand his way of thinking, let me add that he believed we can only think of things that are real: "It is the same thing that can be thought and that can be."[26] So he concludes: Not-being can't be since it can't be thought; and becoming cannot be either since it always starts with not-being. Well, I admit that Parmenides' approach to being and becoming is somewhat tricky. If you haven't got his point yet, just take your time and read this page again. I would like you to actually adopt Parmenides' view of reality for a while in order to comprehend how his ideas were able to influence philosophers in the centuries to come—up to the present day.

Second Challenge: Being and Becoming

Regarding space, Parmenides taught that cosmic space isn't unlimited, but an enormous **sphere** entirely filled with being. This being is the only homogeneous "substance" that permeates all things (including all living things and the air), that our senses perceive in the cosmos, and that constitutes the cosmos itself. In his vision, the cosmos is not composed of temporary objects such as stars, planets, clouds, mountains, or living things that are capable of birth, movement, and death. The entire cosmos would only consist of being, which is one huge, spherical, eternal, motionless substance that is never becoming, but always equal to itself. Whatever we conceive as "becoming" is just an illusion.

I've started this chapter with Parmenides because being seems to be the easiest thing I can understand about myself. I just need to touch my own body—and instantly it feels like "I am." But if I start thinking about the beginning of myself, I soon realize that my life started with becoming, not with being. My mother *became* pregnant with me, I *became* alive, I *became* bigger and bigger. Neither pregnancy, nor birth, nor growing is an eternal, motionless being. And there is more: My senses *became* sharp, my body *became* mature, my brain *became* capable of memory. The becoming of myself continues all of my life until I will *be* (!) dead some day. But if we become day by day, why do we consider ourselves "human beings"—and not "human becomings"? Oops, the spelling program of my laptop is warning me now that the phrase "human becomings" isn't correct.

So, since we are used to consider ourselves human beings, Parmenides' ideas can't be that far off the mainstream. It is reasonable to ask that if something came from nothing, what need could have made it arise later rather than sooner? But in his basic premise, Parmenides definitely misses the truth—we can surely think of something even though it isn't real. Here's one example: I can think of light moving at only one mile per second, but physics tells me that the speed of light is always 186,282 miles per second. Even if light were to *become* slower some day and were to start moving at only one mile per second, Parmenides would have to admit that becoming is part of reality too.

Heraclitus' Fire

We can easily imagine that Parmenides' philosophy was not accepted by everyone, but also provoked a lot of objection. Parmenides' strongest opponent was Heraclitus of Ephesus. Heraclitus believed in a world that's based on becoming, not on being. He thought of the cosmos as a continuously self-igniting **fire:** "The universe, an entity out of everything, has not been made by any god or men; it was, it is, and it will be eternally living fire that is regularly igniting itself and likewise regularly extinguishing itself."[27]

Heraclitus was obsessed with the idea that the world is developing only through contrasts. Any becoming is caused by opposites like day and night, winter and summer, war and peace, satiety and hunger. Yet he also sees harmony in our world—not in an eternal sphere as Parmenides did, but in contrasts: "Men do not know how that which is drawn in different directions harmonizes with itself. The harmony in our world depends upon the tension of opposites like that of

Second Challenge: Being and Becoming

the bow and the lyre."[28] So we would do Heraclitus a great wrong if we reduced his teachings to becoming. While Parmenides objected to any form of becoming, Heraclitus didn't oppose all forms of being. Instead, he claimed that opposites unite to give birth to harmony. I wished that today's nationalists would take this statement to their hearts.

Heraclitus,
Greek philosopher
(sixth/fifth century BC)

One of the most famous sayings by Heraclitus is about life being like a river: "You cannot step twice into the same river."[29] This prominent statement comes with two different interpretations. Most people are aware of only one: If I stroll down the banks of the Mississippi River, the waters before my eyes are permanently changing. So, when stepping into the Mississippi River twice, it can't be the same water—nor the same river—both times. But there is another interpretation to this saying that goes even deeper: I cannot step twice into the Mississippi River since my first bath has somehow changed *myself*. That is to say: I cannot step twice into the same river *as the same person*. Can you hear the bells ringing? Heraclitus is actually telling us that we are becoming anew every single moment that we do something. So, I'm not and never was a human being, but I am and have always been a "human becoming."

Bingo! We are still 500 years before Christ, but we have encountered it again: I am not, yet I become. From now on, this deep *mystic experience* will guide us like a golden thread. I somehow like the image of life being like a river. The peaks and troughs, pits and swirls—they're all part of the ride. So, do as Heraclitus would: Go with the flow and enjoy the ride, as wild as it may be!

Both Parmenides and Heraclitus tried to get to the bottom of our world. Yet, while thinking in terms of being and becoming, they didn't pay much attention to the fact that the world looks different when we change our point of view. Einstein was taking the observer's perspective into account—and his theory holds even more clues for us.

Light's Memory

Let's return to Abraham Lincoln. How could someone claim that he's now seeing him *live* serving as president of the US? Here is the solution: Imagine that our observer is sitting in a spaceship one light-year away from earth. One light-year is the spatial distance that light travels in one year. Let's also assume that our observer has a huge telescope on board and that he is looking through it back to earth. What would he see? He would watch events *live* that had happened on earth precisely one year ago because the light emitted from these events needed one year to reach him. Now, if his spaceship were 60 light-years away from earth, he would see my dear parents *live* marrying although they both already died a few years ago from earth's perspective. So what would he get to see if his spaceship were 158 light-years away from earth? You got it! From there, he would now be watching Abraham Lincoln *live* ruling in White House.

You might argue: What he would get to see is history only. But the clue is: It is history from earth's perspective, but it is *live* from the spaceship's perspective! Here is why: **From my perspective, "history" is anything that happened before "my now"; from my perspective, "live" is anything that's happening at "my now."** So what would our observer see from his spaceship? He wouldn't see a black and white photograph of Abraham Lincoln in an album (figure 14 left); he also wouldn't see any video on DVD. He would indeed watch Abraham Lincoln *live and in full color* (figure 14 right), but from 158 light-years away! He would see him *as live* as you would see me if I were standing ten feet in front of you. If you like football: He would see him *as live* as we would have seen the New England Patriots playing the Philadelphia Eagles on February 4th, 2018, if we had been attending the Super Bowl with binoculars.

Fig. 14: Abraham Lincoln in an album and live in full color

What's going on here? It doesn't really matter whether you watch me *live* from a distance of ten feet, or a football match *live* from a distance of 100 yards, or Abraham Lincoln *live* from a distance of 158 light-years. Spatial distance is the only difference in these three scenarios. And what does this mean in regards to reality? Well, it means that Lincoln isn't president anymore from our perspective, but that he is still president from the perspective of a spaceship 158 light-years away from earth! Both of these perspectives are real. That is: They both describe an event that is happening right *now*, but it depends on an observer's time of what is "now." So, there isn't just one reality in the universe; there are as many realities as there are observers! My reality depends on my space and my time. We can also say: My reality depends on what I read off my ruler and my watch. I know of colleagues who studied Einstein's theory of relativity, but they still can't let go the idea of just one reality. By doing so, they're blocking themselves from the truth.

Now you might ask: If the number of realities is countless, isn't there anything in our world that we may consider as "standing out" from everything else? So let me disclose a great truth to you: Yes, there is! And the big surprise is that it isn't any science fiction. Instead, it is all around us: It's the *light* that we all bathe in. I even go one step further and add: It can't be coincidence that all of our world religions regard light as divine. Here are two examples: Jesus Christ speaks of himself as "the light of the world."[30] Buddhists say about Amida Buddha: "As he is light, so also life, he is eternal."[31] You'll find more examples in my book *How Science Can Help Us Live in Peace*.[32]

Second Challenge: Being and Becoming

So let's talk about light. There is something truly mystical about light: It's the lightest ingredient to the universe. In many languages, including English, "light-ness" is the word itself. English doesn't even distinguish between "light" (in terms of electromagnetic radiation) and "light" (in terms of weight). If you're not yet convinced about light's magic, you might want to consider that, according to basic mechanics, the lightest thing is also the easiest to be moved. So, nothing spreads *easier* than light. Then, based on our experience, we conclude that nothing spreads *faster* than light.

Today, physicists can measure the speed of light very precisely: It is 186,282 miles per second or 670,615,200 miles per hour. We physicists believe that it is a natural constant, that is, light has exactly the same speed everywhere in the cosmos. Yet we're not completely certain of it because we can't measure its speed in the entire cosmos. But we're certain of one thing: Because our human bodies have mass, we can never move at light's speed. This is a profound thing to know. Our own body weight prevents us from keeping up with light, so we can never catch it, let alone understand it. We physicists offer two alternatives—waves and particles—of how to picture the nature of light to ourselves. Yet neither one of these pictures tells the truth. There is, indeed, a very good reason why we will never be able to understand what light truly is: How could we understand something that is too fast to even get ahold of?

So, light is always one step ahead of us. This is another deep mystic experience that reminds us of various religious conceptions of God. We'll soon learn that "always being one step ahead of us" is probably our best option to describe the true nature of light. But for the moment, let's focus on some of the physical properties of light. Besides having a constant speed, light comes with different colors and energy.

When speaking of color, we usually mean visible colors like red and green and blue. Whenever I speak of "light" in this book, I refer to any electromagnetic radiation including the infrared, the radio waves, the ultraviolet, the x-rays, and the gamma rays. All of these waves move at the same speed which we call *speed of light*. In quantum physics, the color of light particles, so-called *photons*, relates to their energy: Blue photons have more energy than green photons; green photons have more energy than red photons.

Light has another feature that is even more fascinating: It transports and gathers information throughout the entire cosmos, and so, it is a **memory** of all that is happening in the cosmos. That's why I called light *cosmic memory*[33] as well as *diary of creation*[34] in one of my earlier books. All things are feeding this cosmic memory by continuously emitting and reflecting light. Our eyes are equipped with special sensors that enable us to decode some of the information contained in the cosmic memory. It's this diary of creation that we look into when watching the stars at night—some of them being 10 billion years old; every star and every planet composes a chapter on its own in the diary of creation. And it's the same memorizing effect of light that makes us see Abraham Lincoln from 158 light-years away. As a matter of fact, Lincoln's presidency becomes accessible *anywhere* in the cosmos if we only wait long enough. And so does anything else! Isn't this amazing? Nothing—not even a blink of my eyes—gets lost because light is involved in everything that happens.

Second Challenge: Being and Becoming

This time you might possibly argue that light can eventually be absorbed by matter. This is absolutely correct, but even so, all the information from our lives can never get lost completely. Why not? Because light doesn't consist of particles or waves that are swallowed up by matter. Instead, light is complex memory that permeates the entire universe and in which every object leaves traces behind (figure 15). Also, information doesn't get lost by being scattered across great distances. All the information is there even if we don't have the technical instruments to decode it. Physically, the range of electromagnetic radiation is infinite.

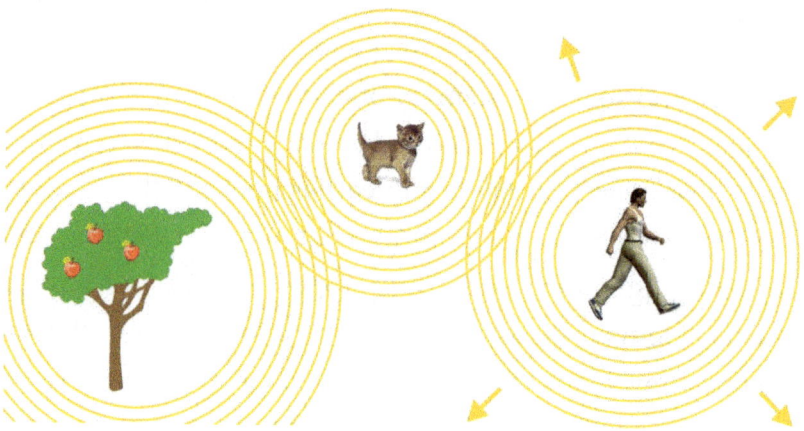

Fig. 15: *Every object leaves traces in the light*

Another interesting feature of light's memory is that the information fed into it can't be erased anymore. This is due to the speed of light. If I wanted to hide some information of my life from light's memory, I couldn't—simply because all the information goes away from my body at a speed that I just can't keep up with. It's a bit like posting something on the *World Wide Web:* Once the information is online, it's put away in so many locations that you can't really get rid of it anymore. The information has already spread in "circles" as in figures 15 and 16. That explains why we're well-advised to describe light as "always being one step ahead of us."

I like to compare the cosmic memory to a book, and we are all authors of this book. Every living thing is writing its pages in this oversized book as it experiences life (figure 16). It knows about these pages and about fragments from other pages, but it doesn't know how its own pages will end, nor does it know the complete book. With this metaphor, I wish to illustrate one important aspect of light's memory: Such a book survives all of its authors—it exists and continues to exist long after its authors have died. So, does light's cosmic memory have the power to conquer death?

Fig. 16: Light as cosmic memory

Second Challenge: Being and Becoming

I then asked myself: "What's so special about light that it serves as cosmic memory? Why can't sound do the job?" As a physicist I found the answer pretty soon: Sound needs a material medium like air or water to transport information from one site to another. Even if we had oversized speakers on earth and shouted something to the moon, an astronaut standing there wouldn't hear us—not because our speakers were too far away, but because there aren't any molecules in empty space that could react to sound and pass it on. So, our shouting would become less and less while passing through earth's atmosphere (figure 17 top). Light is completely different: It moves through anything including empty space. If we had an oversized laser and sent flashes to the moon, our astronaut would receive them, and he could even give us a "thumb up" (figure 17 bottom).

Fig. 17: Propagation of sound versus light (not to scale)

So what are the implications for us, now that we know that light is cosmic memory? Well, here is my advice: Better think twice before you hurt or even kill someone! Whatever misery we do to each other—within the light, actions will be attached to our names for evermore. Wouldn't it be better to have us memorialized with positive things? Cosmic memory gives us this gift too. All we need to do can be summarized in just one sentence: We must give *love and understanding* to each other and to nature herself.

Being and Becoming Are Not Two

I admit having made a mistake myself for several years, and this is the best place and time to correct it. Making mistakes is a human weakness, so please forgive me. I will illustrate my mistake in full detail so that you won't get trapped by it as I was. Unfortunately for themselves, many people don't admit mistakes. Religions, in particular, tend to defend attitudes that science has already unmasked as mistakes.

I was mistaken in believing that light has some point of view or "perspective" to anything in our world. Meanwhile, I have learned that light—although it's an ingredient to our world—cannot have a point of view. We see that immediately if we follow this logical sequence: 1) We'll show that there is no distance (neither spatial nor temporal) *within all light*.[35] 2) From (1) it follows that light is "everywhere" and "anytime." 3) From (2) it follows that there isn't anything light could "look at" or "look forward to." 4) From (3) it follows that light can't have a point of view.

Second Challenge: Being and Becoming

What is distance? A distance separates two events from each other. At the end of the first challenge, I advised you to think of spatial (or temporal) distance as some number that has been given a unit of space (or time, respectively). Now, when we go more into the details, we'll notice that distance is related to *exchanging information*. If we watched Abraham Lincoln from a distance of 158 light-years, we would receive information about his life, but with a *time delay* of 158 years. **"Temporal distance" between two events is the amount of time that is needed to exchange information among them.** In our example, 158 years elapse between "Abraham Lincoln emits light" and "we receive his light." **"Spatial distance" is the same amount of time as in temporal distance, but multiplied by the speed of light.** In our example, it calculates to 158 years x 1 light-year/year, which is 158 light-years. Now, if we were *within* Lincoln's light, there wouldn't be any time delay to exchange that information because it's already with us. And since light is cosmic memory receiving information from all events in the cosmos, the same argument applies to every other information too. That is: Within all light, no time is needed to exchange any information.

We have just shown that there is no distance within all light. Extrapolating the effects of time dilation and length contraction (that we already discussed in our challenge 1) to the speed of light gives us the same result: Within all light, all distances turn zero. This includes temporal and all three spatial distances because, from our perspective, light travels into all of space. Since some physicists limit this statement to just one space dimension in which a light particle is traveling, I decided to emphasize this point here.

We now completed the first step in the logical sequence above. The other three steps follow automatically. So, light can't have a point of view. Today, when looking back, I can say that I was deceived by religious hope: I was hoping that we could live on within the light when we die. But due to its "distancelessness," light isn't a place to live on or to become. Yet light is *the only place to be.* This too fits perfectly to a result from our challenge 1: Light is never aging.

So now we are finally closing the loop that started with Parmenides and Heraclitus—by returning to the two terms that once puzzled them so much: "being" and "becoming." Philosophy always starts with setting up sound definitions. What is it that we're really talking about? Let's give it a first try: "Being" stands for anything that *does not depend on time;* "becoming" stands for anything that *does depend on time.* So, any law of nature is a typical being because it is independent of time; a sunrise or sunset, on the other hand, is a typical becoming.

And how does space relate to being and to becoming? Well, now is the time to fill in our definitions with all that we've learned from Albert Einstein. Always think of space and time as two sides of one and the same coin. So let's improve our original definitions: "Being" stands for anything that *depends on neither space nor time;* "becoming" stands for anything that *depends on space and/or time.*

But still, this isn't the end of our second story and challenge. Einstein also taught us to always think of space and time as adjectives: **"Being" stands for anything that is neither spatial nor temporal; "becoming" stands for anything that is spatial and/or temporal.** So, how do these definitions

57

sound to you? You might argue: In this case, a human *being* couldn't be spatial and temporal, although we know that its body extends into space and ages in time. But please recall: We actually aren't human beings, but "human becomings." So, this example doesn't contradict our definition of being, yet it supports our definition of becoming. This shows how sound our two definitions are. What about a law of nature? It is a being since it is neither spatial nor temporal; it tells us the truth regardless of space and time.

Now we return to the idea of space and time being like playgrounds. According to the definitions that we just came up with, my space and my time make up "my playground of becoming"; it's this playground that we call *reality*. And since every observer has his/her own space and time, he/she has his/her own reality. Being, on the other hand, isn't anything to play with; two plus two is four, and nothing can be done about it. So, being is something very special that truly deserves the name *eternity*. Since light is the only place to be, we finally end up with this definition: **"Eternity" is being within the light.**

Whew! I admit—this was pretty strong stuff. Before inviting you to a short break, let's put our definitions of reality and eternity side by side:

| "Reality" is how I perceive the world in space and time. | "Eternity" is being within the light. |

It's not only all the laws of nature that are stored in the light, but everything that ever is or has ever happened in the cosmos. Please have a break now! I need one too. ☺

Andromeda Galaxy, 2.5 million light-years away from earth

Second Challenge: Being and Becoming

Thanks for joining me again. Now, for the very first time, we are able to "peek" into eternity. Albert Einstein is famous for relating space and time to one another. Yet what most people aren't aware of: Einstein's theory of relativity also leaves plenty of room for "just being" at the speed of light. So now we're ready to face something truly special: the most amazing feature of light.

We are used to think of light as not being connected to "other lights." For instance, we would say: "This is the light from the sun," "that is the light from a candle," and "that is the beam from a flashlight." However, if we insert the speed of light into Einstein's theory of relativity, we find what we just derived before our break: There is no distance within all light. But we've not yet discussed what this statement really means. So let's make up for it now: It means that all light in the universe is actually *one big thing!*

One big thing? No wonder that light rocks our view of a world being clearly separated into "side by side" and "one after another." Just look at figure 18 that displays my wife, our two sons and me—clearly separated from each other by *spatial* distances. You can also see my dear parents smiling warmly at us—they have been *temporally* separated from us since their death. Next, please compare figure 18 to figure 19 that shows various moments of our lives captured for eternity. You see these situations as "drops" because Alfred North Whitehead—for me, one of the smartest philosophers ever—will tell us in a later chapter that our world is actually made up of "drops of experience." It's easy to see why figure 19 is my favorite in this book. It reminds me: "No moment that I shared with my loved ones will ever be forgotten."

Being and Becoming Are Not Two

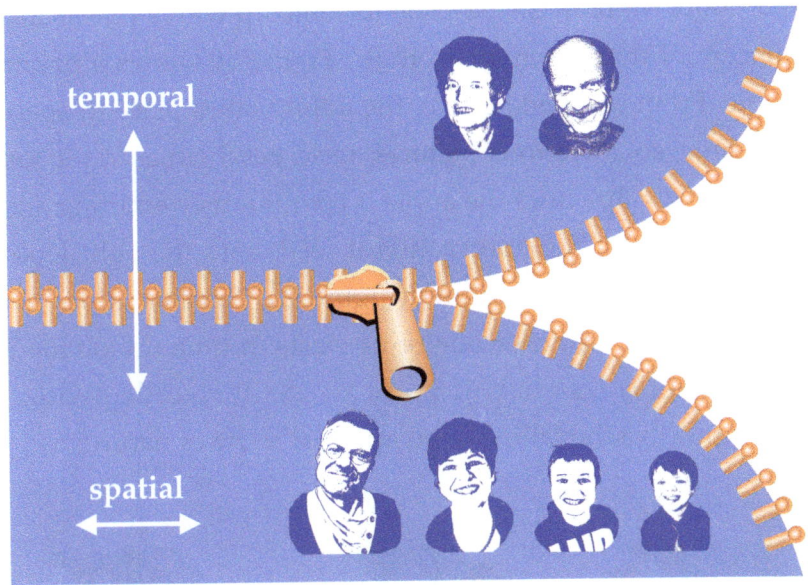

Fig. 18: *My reality splits in space and time*

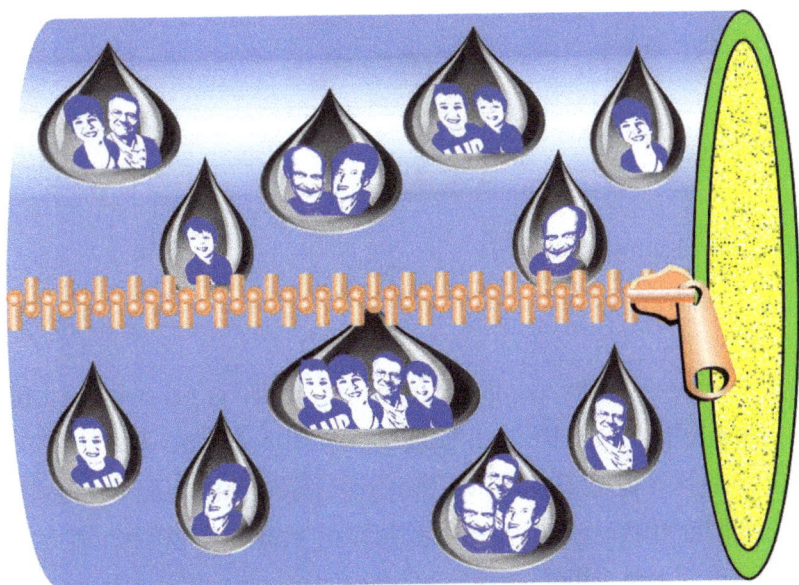

Fig. 19: *Eternity embraces all moments of my life*

Second Challenge: Being and Becoming

Now we're in the position to come up with a reasonable concept of the adjective "eternal." Figure 20 shows a falling apple. From our perspective, the falling takes place in space and time; so, if we took pictures, we'd get them as at the top of figure 20. But since the apple is continuously emitting and reflecting light, the information it feeds into the light looks like the data at the bottom of figure 20. "Eternal" does not mean that the apple or one of us exists in time unbounded. **Something is "eternal" if it can always be recalled within the light** (like the falling of an apple or a law of nature).

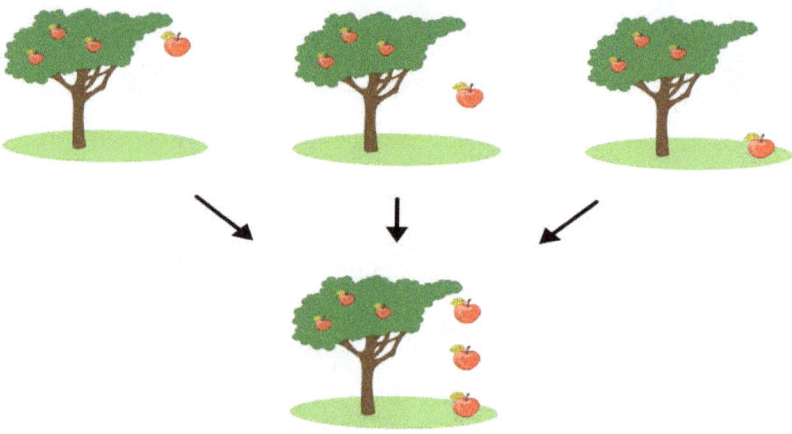

Fig. 20: A blink in eternity

Since eternity is all about being, there is no past and no future to it. Everything is just there—there is no sequence to it. Did you already notice that the page numbers are missing? I let them go to add a touch of eternity. Austrian poet Rainer Maria Rilke wrote: "Cancel the count!"[36] We are on the wrong track if we think that space and time are real, but eternity is an illusion. It's the other way around: Space and time *alone* are illusions as they exist only *together*; eternity is real. Yet how can eternity gather information if there is no past and no future? The answer: From our perspective, we gradually add information to the cosmic memory—one by one. But within all light, when there is no distance, all of our time elapses "at once." Everything is just there, even every position of a falling apple. We compared cosmic memory to an oversized book. From our perspective, the book is *becoming;* our writing is dynamic. Within all light, the book *just is;* light memorizes everything that happens. We contribute to the becoming of the cosmos; the light scripts everything that ever is or has ever happened in the cosmos.

So, which comes first—being or becoming? In this challenge, we've learned that there is "being" and "becoming" in the cosmos. Since neither of these terms makes sense on its own, they require each other. That is why neither being nor becoming comes first.

> Message of our second challenge:
> *There is no being without becoming,*
> *and no becoming without being.*
>
> Alternative ways to express this message:
> *Being and becoming are not two.*
> *Being and becoming are two sides of the same coin.*
>
> The coin's name is: *cosmos.*

Third Challenge:
Good and Evil

Third Challenge: Good and Evil

Which Comes First—Good or Evil?

> ORDER IS RHYTHM AND HARMONY,
> CHANCE IS VARIATION AND MELODY.
> THEY MOVE AS ONE.

In the fourteenth century, a pious doctor helped thousands of Europeans in fighting Black Death, but one day he picked it up himself. So he prayed to God: "I've been so good to all these fellows—please kill those demons inside of me and let me finish my sacred work!" God answered: "Good old man, what demons are you talking about?" The weakened doctor whispered: "All those creatures that squeeze life out of our bodies." God eased his pain, but spoke: "I understand what you're saying, good man, yet both of my hands are tied. My right hand won't move because laws of nature can't be bypassed; unlike man-made laws they make no exceptions. My left hand won't move because I'm not taking sides; I'm also God to those creatures inside of you." The man could hardly express himself: "So what can I do?" God advised him not to send a prayer of petition, but a prayer of thanks.

This short anecdote addresses major points of our third challenge: the relativity of good and evil, determination and freedom in nature, the impossibility of being almighty, the true purpose of praying. At first glance, God's advice seems to lack empathy, but we'll soon learn how wise it actually is. Life comes with all the ingredients of a good game: There is *order* that provides life with rhythm and harmony; we feel good if our cells are in harmony. How chaotic life would be if there were no such thing as order! And there is *chance* that lets life choose from variation and melody. How boring life would be if there were no such thing as chance!

Both order and chance are essential for life to prosper. We now need to set up sound definitions as we did before: **Something happens "by order" if something else causes it to happen; something happens "by chance" if it happens by itself.** An example of order would be: Gravity causes ripe apples to fall down to the ground. Examples of chance are harder to find because it can be very challenging to rule out any cause. Many physicists cite radioactivity as an example of chance because they believe that it occurs randomly. But the truth is: As of today, we aren't aware of any cause; there might be a cause of radioactivity that we haven't discovered yet. This explains why many people don't believe in chance. They assume that every event is caused by something else — even if they can't tell us what it is. Well, here is my advice: Let's finish this third challenge and find out whether there is chance or not. While doing so, we will also learn about good and evil, and how they relate to one another.

Leibniz' Theodicy

We already met German polymath Gottfried Wilhelm Leibniz when discussing Clarke's bucket. Do you remember? It was Leibniz who insisted that space can't be absolute. But his thoughts weren't limited to space and time. He was an all-in-one: philosopher, mathematician, historian, and theo-

Third Challenge: Good and Evil

logian. Leibniz is very well known for having developed the basic ideas of differential and integral calculus. But Leibniz also coined a term that keeps our theologians on the run up to the present day: **theodicy.** The term "theodicy" is derived from the Greek words *theos* (English: God) and *dike* (English: justice). That is: Theodicy questions the justification of a God since there are both good and evil in our world. In his work *Essais de Théodicée sur la bonté de Dieu,* Leibniz comes up with a distinct answer: God doesn't underachieve in creating our world because it is the best of all possible worlds.[37] That is to say: God can't be blamed for all the evil because there is no better world than ours.

Gottfried Wilhelm Leibniz,
German polymath
(1646 – 1716)

Essais de Théodicée was the only book-length treatise that Leibniz published during his life. This illustrates the significance that he attributed to the topic. Leibniz gave us a deep theological puzzle, and with it he hits all religions very hard that acknowledge a God of creation: Judaism, Christianity, and Islam. This is because these three religions proclaim that God *created* our world with all the good and bad sides of life. So it's very reasonable for believers to ask in dismay: If there is a God, how can he/she/it permit the manifestation of evil? Why won't he/she/it do anything about it?

Leibniz' Theodicy

To fully understand Leibniz' point of view, we need to go deeper into his conception of God. His premises are: God is *all-powerful, all-knowing, and all-good*. Under these assumptions, we must be living in the best of all worlds, right? But philosophical conclusions frequently break down because of their premises. Leibniz' premises run into trouble too. We'll see next why there can't be an all-powerful God, no matter how much we might wish that it could be so.

Being all-powerful is a question of freedom. If there is a God, how free can he/she/it be? Does God have the freedom to override laws of nature and chance? It turns out that "all-powerful" is a very problematic concept because it contains a hidden reference to itself. Whoever has power over something restricts freedom of that something. An all-powerful God could force its power upon everything, including upon itself. And so, God would deprive itself of its own freedom! But the opposite should be the case: An all-powerful God, of course, should have *all* power to provide itself with unlimited freedom. The only way out of this logical contradiction is to surrender the concept of an all-powerful God.

The greatest pitfall of Judaism, Christianity, and Islam might be that they won't let go of an all-powerful God. For instance, *El Shaddai* (English: God almighty) is one of many names of the Jewish God. The Christian creed begins with: "I believe in God, the father *almighty*, creator of heaven and earth..."[38] Millions of believers repeat these words without being aware that God may not live up to their expectations. And Muslims believe in almightiness too: "Those who don't call upon Allah for his help wouldn't be able to make even a tiny fly... Allah is indeed strong and *all-powerful.*"[39]

Third Challenge: Good and Evil

In our age of information, there are more and more followers with a tremendous thirst for answers. If they are told to believe in an all-powerful God, of course, they would like to know why this God won't do anything about the evil. The longer that they are made to wait for answers, the more they will turn away from their religions and look for alternatives. The future of Judaism, Christianity, and Islam will depend on whether they can solve Leibniz' theodicy and how they can deal with it. The most honest way would be: "We admit that 'all-powerful' is an attribute imputed to God by God-fearing believers a long time ago. It was meant to intimidate people to make them live in peace. But since this attribute contradicts all logic, we refrain from using it anymore."

Yet I'm afraid that today's religious leaderboard won't admit that they had been mistaken in this point; it's the most difficult thing for humans to admit mistakes. This is so sad because we can learn only from our mistakes. Another issue is that most people find it difficult to let power go. Admitting mistakes always comes with a lack of power.

Followers will be relieved when they hear that religious beliefs, too, may be scrutinized. A dogma that must not be questioned isn't worthy of being followed. Leibniz deserves credit for having brought up the issue of theodicy, but he's guilty of not having proven that our world really is the best. Whoever has experienced onslaughts of fate can easily imagine other worlds where things go far better for him and his loved ones. Most likely, Leibniz was blinded by his own conception of God to see this. If an all-good God exists, there is only one answer to the theodicy: God can't intervene *into* our world because God isn't *outside* of our world.

Laplace's Demon

Roughly 100 years after Leibniz died, French mathematician Pierre-Simon Laplace was the first to publish the articulation of a causal determinism. In his lecture notes *A Philosophical Essay On Probabilities*, he made this statement: "An intellect who at a certain moment would know all forces that set nature in motion, and all positions of all items of which nature is composed, if this intellect were also vast enough to submit these data to analysis, it would embrace in a single formula the movements of the greatest bodies of the universe and those of the tiniest atom; for such an intellect nothing would be uncertain and the future just like the past would be present before its eyes."[40]

Pierre-Simon Laplace,
French mathematician
(1749 – 1827)

Laplace himself doesn't speak of a "**demon**," but this is exactly what his words imply: If an "intellect" (the demon) knew the precise location of every atom in the universe and all the forces acting upon it, then the past and future of all atoms would be determined; the demon could calculate all values from the laws of mechanics. So, Laplace is saying that if such data of all atoms were accessible, then the world and all of its life would be predestined. And if the world were predestined, then it wouldn't be given any chance to become better. How could there be a "better world" if there were no variation at all? So, Laplace is blowing away Leibniz' theory of "the best of all worlds" by claiming that there is only one world. But for his demon, we all would have to pay a very high price: We wouldn't have any freedom at all.

Laplace's demon wandered like a ghost through scientist's minds until Henri Poincaré, also French mathematician and physicist, showed that mankind can't predict the future, by making a major contribution[41] to the so-called *three-body problem*. I will shorten it for you: Is it possible to calculate the orbits of three planets for all of time in the past and future if they interact with each other? Poincaré showed that the orbits can't be calculated *analytically* (that is, from a formula) although they are all determined by the laws of mechanics; we can only *approximate* the orbits. So, since the approximations are very sensitive to small variations of the initial values and since we can't precisely measure these initial values, mankind isn't able to predict the future for all of time.

But if mankind can't predict the future, what about demons? Could a demon predict the future? It was in the 1920s when quantum theory finally got rid of the spook. According to a fundamental principle of this theory known as *Heisenberg's uncertainty principle* (we will meet Werner Heisenberg in our next challenge), an atom is not given both a precise location and a precise velocity[42] at the same time. So, it is not our instruments that prevent us from measuring the exact values—the uncertainty is anchored in nature herself. There is no way that anyone (including a demon) could precisely determine the initial values of all atoms because they don't exist. And that's why no one can predict the future for all of time. Laplace recognized the *significance of determinism;* Poincaré demonstrated that *mankind* isn't able to predict the future for all of time; Heisenberg showed the *general inability* to predict the future for all of time. One guy was never convinced by quantum physics: Einstein said that God wouldn't play dice.[43] And yet, it's precisely this uncertainty that opens the doors for nature to "play" with freedom!

Before we proceed with our next step, we need to do some extra brainstorming: We must understand the big difference between events *happening by chance* and events *being unpredictable*. Most people confuse these two terms. Gambling for instance is never by chance, but always unpredictable, provided that the game isn't manipulated. Whatever side a dice will rest upon and into whatever slot a roulette ball will fall into is determined by mechanical forces. But the process is so complex that we just can't predict the outcome. Likewise, so-called *random number generators* (computer programs that produce a series of random numbers) don't generate chance. Chance can't be generated since it's acting alone. We already consider numbers as *random* if their generation is so complex that we can't predict the next number.

So let's now start talking about chance. Chance is from a superior quality: Whatever happens by chance is a creative act *in itself* since it isn't caused by anything else. Something completely new is created that can't be derived from history alone. There is, indeed, something "very special" happening whenever we see true chance at work. In our fifth challenge, Alfred North Whitehead will share with us what this "very special" is all about. But for now, we're all set to resume our philosophical journey. Coming up next, I invite you to read about a surprising experiment performed a few decades ago that still puzzles scientists, philosophers, and theologians all the way up to the Vatican.

Libet's Experiment

In the year 1983, an American physiologist published results of a new kind of **experiment** that started an intense debate about free will. His name: Benjamin Libet. Libet studied the chronology of events during the decision-making process in human brains. The results surprised him and his team and, to this day, cause lively discussions throughout the civilized world. In order to interpret them proficiently, let's first get familiar with the experimental setup.

Libet's experiment is sketched in figure 21. A subject is sitting in an armchair and looks at a large clock with a green point making one revolution in approximately 2.5 seconds.[44] Electric sensors are connected to the subject's head and right wrist. They measure brain activity and muscle activity in the right hand, respectively. The subject is given this instruction: "Watch the green point on that clock. Move your right hand at any time when you feel the urge to do so. Note to yourself where exactly the green point is at this point in time." After completing the task, the subject is asked by Libet where the green point was located on the large clock when he/she felt the urge to move the hand. Libet compares this point in time with the onset of brain and muscle activities.

Libet's Experiment

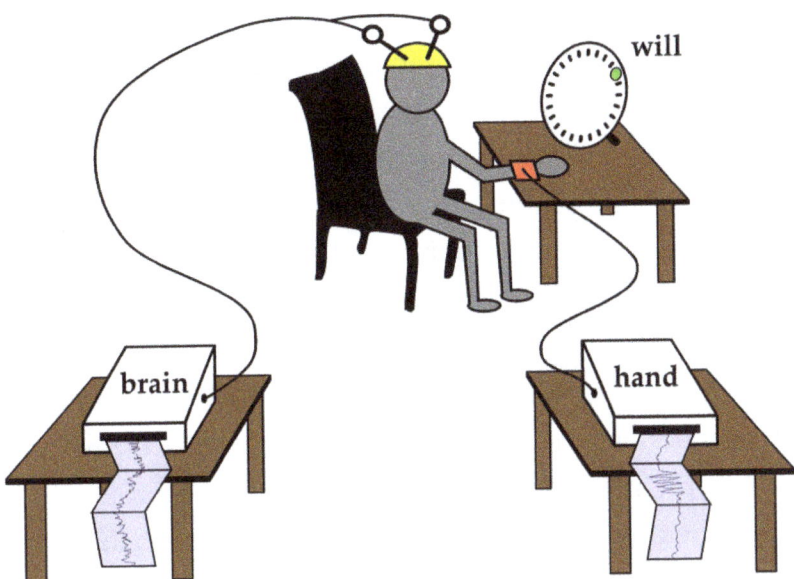

Fig. 21: Libet's experiment

Now let's see what Libet measured during his original experiment. Figure 22 shows all recorded events on a single time scale: t_{brain} is the point in time when brain activity was increased; t_{will} indicates the point in time when the subject felt the urge to move the hand; and t_{hand} marks the point in time when the hand actually moved.

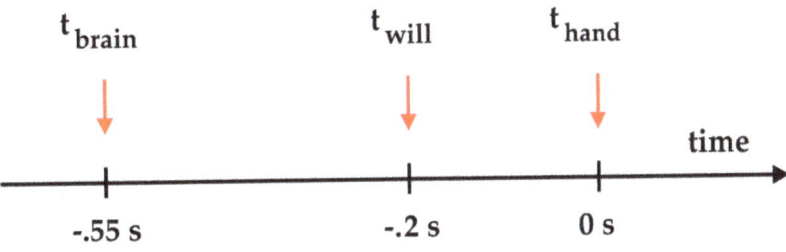

Fig. 22: Events during Libet's experiment

Third Challenge: Good and Evil

And indeed, at first glance, this finding comes as a big surprise. One of Libet's observations makes good sense: The subject's hand didn't move until .2 seconds after the point in time that the subject felt the urge to do so; this delay might be due to the amount of time necessary for the stimulus to transfer from the brain to the wrist. But why did brain activity increase long *before* the subject had the will to move the hand? Did something else anticipate that decision? Was the subject not free to decide for himself/herself when to move the hand? Libet never questioned the existence of free will, but his findings are often interpreted to that effect.

However, jumping to conclusions based on this interpretation would be premature because of the experimental setup and the difficulty in evaluating the exact time of when the subject actually decides to move the hand. Please recall: The subjects were asked to memorize the point in time when they "felt the urge" to move their hand. This point in time merely indicates when a subject *became conscious* of the urge. It does not match the point in time when he or she *had made the decision* to move the hand! So, our will can indeed be free, but we become conscious of the decisions that we make only with a temporal delay.

Meanwhile, scientists have repeated Libet's experiment and have added several improvements. It was argued that the brain activity measured by Libet couldn't have caused the hand to move. A modified experiment shows this activity even if the subject quickly decides not to move the hand.[45] So, this activity merely indicates the subject's readiness for a forthcoming motion, and that's why experts[46] call it *readiness potential*. Libet was also criticized for not giving his subjects any true freedom of choice. The only freedom that they had was whether they would like to participate in his study or not; but by participating, each subject was required to move the hand at some time or other. In a follow-up experiment, the subject was given the additional freedom to move either the right or left pointing finger.[47] Again, the readiness potential was active before the subject became conscious of his/her decision, but the measured activity didn't disclose the final choice of the subject.

All these results are the subject of live controversy even today. Scientists agree that most activities in the brain occur *unconsciously* and that consciousness is built[48] from the unconscious. Libet's work supports this claim by showing that the conscious mind lags behind. But scientists still disagree on the freedom of the unconscious since we have no control of anything that we aren't aware of. I believe that the unconscious is a key to understanding ourselves. More and more people shut themselves off from others because they superficially identify themselves only with their bodies and their consciousness. They're blind to how we all affect each other. If these people had access to the unconscious that connects us altogether, they wouldn't shut themselves off.

It really surprises me how Libet's experiment was able to cause such a sensation at all. Wouldn't a disproof of free will add fuel to our materialistic world? The passion thrown in to defend the existence of free will speaks for itself. Is our will free or not free? The correct answer to this question is so crucial for understanding life that I have a little task for you: Please start reading this important chapter *Libet's Experiment* again. Do not read any further—whatever happens!

At the risk of being blamed
for wasting two pages of this book—
I just asked you to not read any further.

Please go back to
the start of the chapter *Libet's Experiment*
even if you have already read it several times!

Third Challenge: Good and Evil

So now you see . . . thank you for participating in this little experiment! Actually, you would have never been permitted to read this very page because I had emphatically told you to not read any further. You even ignored my second warning when I expressly asked you to return to the start of this chapter again and again.

Well, you are reading these lines now. You have your free will to thank for this. It really was *you* who decided not to follow my request. You decided it *consciously* and *from out of your own*. In other words: You made use of your free will! If you now reflect on what had happened during these past minutes, you'll probably agree that there was some *sudden* moment when you decided that the task given to you was silly and that you want to turn the page. It was a *spontaneous* decision that just popped up "out of the blue." Sudden and spontaneous—these are perhaps the best attributes that we have in our language to describe chance. They express what chance is all about: Something happens by itself. It can't be made any clearer than what you just experienced yourself. Our will is free, and so, it's a valid example of chance.

Any archaic computer would have got hung up in such a loop and crashed. In computer science, this is called *infinite loop*. Computers just go along their merry way and carry out one command after another. They aren't able to escape from such an infinite loop on their own unless they have the latest upgrade to automatically exit the loop after a set amount of time. But our little experiment didn't have any set amount of time that was preprogrammed so that you could escape the loop. It only had one "emergency exit," and it was you who used it: your free will!

So, there's no need to build a big machine to prove that our will is free. All it needs is a creative idea. I even believe that our experiment is superior to Libet's setup because the only way to verify spontaneity is *to experience it yourself,* and this is precisely what you just did. Now we still need to investigate whether there are more random forces in the universe other than free will and how they relate to the theme of our third challenge: good and evil. This is what we will be doing next. Relax and enjoy!

Good and Evil Are Not Two

Now that we've discovered chance, we're faced with events in the universe that aren't predestined. So, there is no such demon as Laplace spoke about. Scientists assume that there are, indeed, quite a few examples of chance in the universe: The very first example was presumably the *big bang* 14 billion years ago when cosmic energy suddenly expanded and cooled off to form matter.[49] My second example is *spontaneous breaking of symmetry* by which a system in a symmetric state ends up in an asymmetric state.[50] The third example is *radioactivity* if it really turns out not to have a cause.[51] My next example is the *beginning of life.* Just imagine! Out of the blue, matter arranges itself to form clusters that are alive.[52] Beginning of life is very typical of chance because matter can be either not alive or alive, and there is nothing in between; so, the transition from one to the other must be spontaneous. My fifth example is *free will,* which isn't limited to mankind, but is also shared among higher animals. I can think of one

Third Challenge: Good and Evil

more example, which even shows us that chance is at work everywhere in the universe: the *spontaneous emission of light*. Excited atoms spontaneously emit light upon returning to a lower energy level.[53] This is similar to the beginning of life: The energy is either still in the atom or it has already left the atom, and there is nothing in between; so, this kind of transition must be spontaneous too.

Let's summarize what we know by now: There is both chance and order. Something happening by chance happens by itself; something happening by order is caused by something else, but caused events seem at times unpredictable for us. We've also learned that chance is at work everywhere in the universe. The same is true for order: Laws of nature are in effect everywhere as well. So, since order and chance are the basic ingredients to any good game, the evolution of the universe (and this includes the evolution of life) may indeed be considered a game.

In a game, we tend to speak of "good moves" and "bad moves." So, good and evil are qualities of *progress*. A move can be either good or bad for me as a player, or it turns out to be irrelevant for me. A game is progressing due to order and/or chance, but progress in any game is neither good nor evil in itself; it is only interpreted as "good" or "evil" by the effect that it has upon us. **"Good" is anything that improves things from my perspective; "evil" is anything that makes things worse from my perspective.** There is no absolute evil and no absolute good. Good and evil are relative qualities like space and time. We only need to switch sides to see that: An antibiotic is good for us, but the same antibiotic is evil for some kinds of bacteria.

Let's find more examples that illustrate the relativity of good and evil. If you left a sinking boat and couldn't swim, you could *drown* in water; but if you wandered in a hot desert and had thirst, water could keep you *alive*.

If you were the one who lost 50 dollars in the subway this morning, you would be *annoyed* by the loss; but if you were the lucky one to find these 50 dollars, someone else's loss would *make your day*.

If you like football and were a fan of the New England Patriots, the Super Bowl on February 4th, 2018, would *not be* a good thing to remember; but if you were a fan of the Philadelphia Eagles, the same Super Bowl would be a *highlight* in your life.

For teenagers who would like to have all the options of an adult, *being older* would be a good thing; for older people who would like to climb the trees once more, *being younger* would be a good thing.

At my readings, I am regularly asked why some people can live happy lives with good outcomes while others experience onslaughts of fate such as a severe illness, an accident, a natural disaster, a school shooting, or a terrorist attack. My answer is the same in all of these cases: Progress in the game of life is neither good nor evil in itself. It always results from order (laws of nature, social environment, lifestyle, viruses, bacteria) and/or chance (radioactivity can trigger the growth of cancer; by chance I can be at the wrong place at the wrong time—for example, by making use of my free will). The fate of each of our lives is not predestined. It is in the hands of order and chance. There is no deeper meaning to experiencing onslaughts of fate.

Third Challenge: Good and Evil

There is no doubt that good and evil are challenging us each day of our lives. It's not surprising that believers pray to their God for shelter. But we already discussed Leibniz' theodicy and found that there is no God who could override laws of nature and chance. This has profound consequences: If God can't stop evil, then prayers of petition are pointless. Prayers of petition can't make things any better, but at best they can offer comfort to those who pray. Praying is helpful for turning inwardly and for understanding that God is not taking sides with anyone or anything. We ask the *impossible* of God if we ask him/her/it to assist us in our fight against bacteria and/or cancer cells. How could God take sides if he/she/it is God to all living things including bacteria and cancer cells? Some of us never ask God for help, but instead *thank* God for being alive. "Prayers of thanks" were the first prayers ever uttered by living things. Whoever gives thanks holds himself/herself back. By doing so, he/she achieves the greatest of all: He/she surrenders!

Do you still remember how we got started in this book? "When you wish to find a clue, try to change your point of view!" This wise saying can also help us cope with strokes of fate. Bring every precious moment in life to your mind by realizing how it stands out from the hard times. And on the other hand, if you are experiencing hard times, bring to your mind that we must experience these, too, to cherish the good times. Just think about it: How could we ever cherish health if we had never experienced illness before? And how could we ever cherish the good sides of life if we had never experienced its bad sides before? There is no good without evil, and no evil without good.

What about "good people" and "bad people"? Recently, Donald Trump spoke of "really bad people" coming into the US from the Mexican border.[54] Would we all be "really bad people" if we had been born in countries that don't guarantee a human life? Certainly not. No one is born as a culprit. It's the environment we live in that makes us who we are! *No one is an island; no one is good or bad alone.* I hope so much that people on earth can see the difference between the truth and words that are only sold as the truth. We all are responsible for humankind. It's not the "bad guy" with a gun, who is responsible for a school shooting. All those of us are responsible, who didn't think that it was necessary to help this guy and who contributed to letting him wear a gun. We all have heard the manufacturers of weapons say: "You need a weapon to defend yourself!" But what if there is no yourself to defend? What if there is only an ourselves as we'll learn in our next challenge? In that case, I'm afraid, our weapons will be killing ourselves.

Message of our third challenge:
There is no good without evil,
and no evil without good.

Alternative ways to express this message:
Good and evil are not two.
Good and evil are two sides of the same coin.

The coin's name is: *progress*.

I'M SURE YOU HAVE NOTICED THAT THIS BOOK IS DIFFERENT.
IT'S UNIQUE AND POWERFUL IN WHAT IT HAS TO SAY.

NOW IT'S HALFTIME OF OUR PHILOSOPHICAL JOURNEY.
THIS BOOK IS ALSO UNIQUE IN TAKING ADVANTAGE
OF THIS PROMINENT BREAK TO LET ME SAY THANKS:

MY DEAR ALEXANDRA FOR BEING THE SUNSHINE IN MY LIFE,
DEAR JOSUA AND SAMUEL FOR BEING THE BLOSSOMS OF MY LIFE,
DEAR MOM AND DAD FOR HAVING BEEN THE ROOTS OF MY LIFE.

THIS TIME MY VERY SPECIAL THANKS GO TO JIM
FOR SHARING SO MANY WISE COMMENTS WITH ME.
YOU ARE THE BEST TRANSLATOR I COULD HAVE FOUND.
JIM, THIS IS OUR BOOK FOR THE WELL-BECOMING OF MANKIND.

YOUR COSMIC BROTHER,
MARKOLF

Fourth Challenge: Chicken and Egg

Fourth Challenge: Chicken and Egg

Which Comes First—the Chicken or the Egg?

> LIFE IS ABOUT LEARNING,
> NOT ABOUT WINNING.

When I look at humankind today, I have the uncomfortable feeling that most people care about their money and profit, but not about how everyone can live in true harmony with nature. This is so sad because money and profit can't buy a new earth to live on. If we continue to ruin our planet and don't succeed in colonizing other planets, we'll have wiped out ourselves. The evolution of life will move past us if we aren't smart enough to keep up with nature.

So let's talk about ourselves and the evolution of life. A straight way into the topic is a riddle that was already posed in the first century AD by the Greek writer Plutarch: Which comes first—the chicken or the egg?[55] In those days, it was common belief that everything on earth and in the sky had been individually created by Gods: Sheep as sheep, birds as birds. People had no idea that millions of species have been evolving on our planet throughout billions of years.

Plutarch's riddle addresses the relation of parent and child. Generally speaking, it addresses the relation of cause and effect. The riddle itself holds both a hint and a trick for us. The word "comes" leads us into the right direction: The solution must be *dynamic*. But then the word "first" puts us on the wrong track. As we will see in this fourth challenge, there's neither "the chicken" nor "the egg"; the chickens that

Which Comes First—the Chicken or the Egg?

live on earth today are genetically different from those that lived a few hundred or a million years ago. The same is true for eggs. Chickens and eggs have never stopped evolving. In one of my earlier books,[56] I recommended speaking of verbs ("chicken-ing," "egg-ing"). The disadvantage of our nouns is that they cover up what life is all about—unfolding! So, the solution to Plutarch's riddle is of the same type again: Neither chicken nor egg comes first (figure 23).

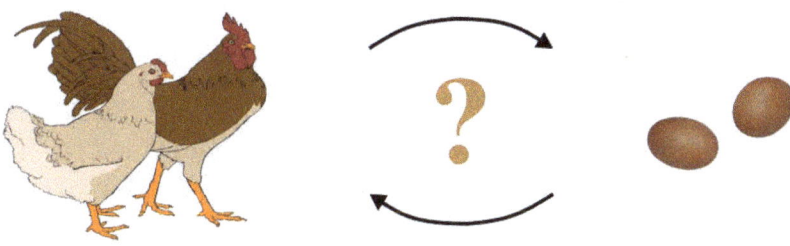

Fig. 23: Which comes first—the chicken or the egg?

I wonder why mankind can't help thinking in terms of "being first." We'll soon learn that the evolution of life isn't based on such concepts as "being first" or "being strongest." Life is about learning, not about winning. But the news that we get to watch is often about being first or being strongest: the *first* company to reach $1 trillion market value, the *richest* man or woman, the world *champions* in some kind of sports. Who cares about those who are second or third or last? We could easily slow down the race for being number one if we only wanted to—by doing better in regulating free markets, by listening to those who aren't on the winning side of life, and by making way for sports that have only winners.

Fourth Challenge: Chicken and Egg

Cuvier's Fossils

English naturalist Charles Darwin was the first to publish a theory of evolution based on *natural selection,* but the idea of evolving species had already been brought up by others. It dates back to the sixth century BC when Greek philosopher Anaximander taught that mankind emerged from "fishlike animals."[57] Two centuries later, Greek philosopher Aristotle observed animals in the Mediterranean Sea and set up the first model of evolution.[58]

In the eighteenth century AD, it was French naturalist Georges Cuvier who made several contributions to biology. He founded *vertebrate paleontology,* and he confirmed for the first time that biological species can become extinct.[59] Studying **fossils** was the key to his success.

Georges Cuvier,
French naturalist
(1769 – 1832)

In his *Essay on the Theory of the Earth,* Cuvier writes of his paleontological technique: "The form of the tooth leads to the form of the condyle, that of the scapula to that of the nails ... The nails, the scapula, the condyle, the femur, each separately reveal the tooth or each other. And by beginning from each of them, the thoughtful professor of the laws of organic economy can reconstruct the entire animal."[60]

Yet Cuvier was very critical of theories of evolution. His work with fossils made him believe that one form of a bone does not gradually transform into a distinct form. His goal was to create accurate taxonomy of life that would be based on true comparative anatomy, but such a project would fail if biological species were continually mutating. Cuvier considered an animal to be a functional whole. If any part of the animal were modified, the whole animal would die because all of its parts are interdependent. This clearly demonstrates that Cuvier did not believe in evolution of any kind. But he deserves credit for having developed a classification scheme for animals[61] that is still in use today.

Lamarck's Giraffes

French Jean-Baptiste Lamarck started his scientific career as a botanist, but in 1793 he became one of the cofounders of the *Muséum National d'Histoire Naturelle* in Paris as an expert on invertebrates (spineless animals). His work on classifying worms, spiders, molluscs, and other boneless creatures was far ahead of his time.

Jean-Baptiste Lamarck,
French naturalist
(1744 – 1829)

Fourth Challenge: Chicken and Egg

Lamarck spotted numerous similarities among animals and concluded that life must be very flexible. Organisms are able to *adapt* to a changing environment in order to survive. If an animal used a specific organ more often than it had in the past, then that organ would adapt by increasing in size. If a **giraffe** stretched its neck to reach high leaves, Lamarck believed that a "nervous fluid" would flow into its neck and make it a bit longer[62] (figure 24). Its offspring would inherit the elongated neck, and further stretching would make the neck even longer. In the meantime, other parts of the body that the animals stopped using would shrink.

Fig. 24: *Lamarck's giraffes*

The "nervous fluid" postulated by Lamarck was never found, and so, his studies were ignored or even mocked by others. Lamarck realized the significance of adaptation, but he was wrong in explaining how adaption truly takes place. A few more years went by until someone else came up with that explanation: Charles Darwin.

Darwin's Tree of Life

Hardly any scientist questioned our role in the cosmos more profoundly than English naturalist Charles Darwin. After aborting his medical education, he first became a theologian. Darwin was deeply influenced by the natural philosophy of his countryman William Paley who is known for his watchmaker analogy: A designed world implies a designer—God! Darwin devoured Paley's book *Natural Theology*.[63]

Charles Darwin,
English naturalist
(1809 – 1882)

It was a stroke of fate for science when the twenty-two year old Darwin was invited to take part in a circumnavigation of the globe. In December 1831, the young theologian launched to sea aboard the *HMS Beagle.* At first, he believed that God had created every kind of living thing *individually.* But after traveling oceans and continents, his observations of nature gave him an entirely different picture: He discovered sea fossils at an altitude of 12,000 feet on mountains in South America, he found biological relationships among remotely isolated turtles living on the Galapagos islands, and he preserved 1,529 different biological species including a group of finch-like songbirds that he also observed on the Galapagos islands.[64]

After his return in October 1836, he sent his collected items to John Gould at the museum of the *Zoological Society of London*.[65] Gould investigated the birds and confirmed that there was no clear separation among them: They were uniformly joined in every way. Darwin himself didn't give the birds any special notice during his return trip to England. Of course, the different shapes of their beaks (figure 25) did not escape Darwin, but these shapes only reinforced his opinion that all his finches represented different species.

Fig. 25: Darwin's finches

Only after long conversations with Gould was Darwin compelled to come up with his revolutionary interpretation of the different finch beaks. The birds adapted to the various food resources that were available to them on the separated islands: big beaks for grains, sharp beaks for insects! Yet the adaptation wasn't caused by a "nervous fluid," but a process that Darwin coined *natural selection*.[66] Only birds with the right beak were able to survive; others became extinct. Darwin's finches are a classic example of *adaptive radiation*: An original species adapts to its environment by branching into highly specialized species. Grain-eating finches, insect-eating finches, woodpecker finches, and others[67] branched from only a few original finches on the Galapagos islands (figure 26). Woodpecker finches, for example, use tiny twigs as tools to remove larvae from tree bark. In this way, nature is very successful in making use of ecological niches. Today, we can say that the great distances among the small Galapagos islands actually favored the development of new species because most of the animals living on one particular island weren't able to cross over to a different island.

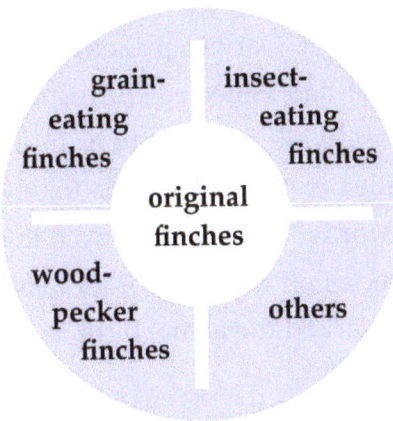

Fig. 26: An example of adaptive radiation

The beaks of finch-like songbirds were just a small part of the jig-saw puzzle of Darwin's reasoning. Taken together, all the pieces added up to form a big picture that refuted all creation biology valid at that time. Biological species are not changeless living things that had been created individually by a "God of creation," but they develop gradually through the long process of natural selection: Only those species survive that have learned to live in harmony with nature!

Another twenty years went by until Darwin published his life's work in November 1859: *On the Origin of Species.*[68] He made five revolutionary claims in this book:

– the changeability of all species,
– creation of species in minute progressions,
– propagation of species within populations,
– the common origin of all forms of life,
– natural selection as the pivotal mechanism of life.

To further support these claims, Darwin presented detailed scientific evidence that he had collected during and following the return of his worldwide investigation. In his *Notebook B*,[69] he sketched his idea of the **tree of life** for the first time. Beginning with his words "I think" follows a tree that displays the biological species on the ends of its many branches (figure 27). This idea marked the actual birth of the theory of evolution.

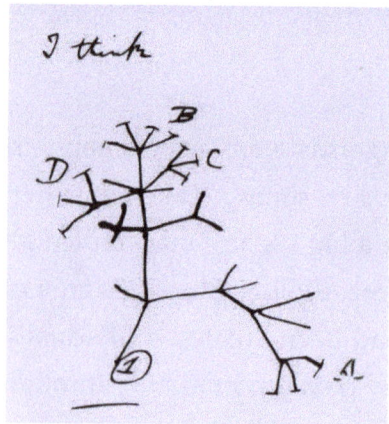

Fig. 27: Darwin's first sketch of the tree of life

Darwin does not express any kind of special role that mankind might have in his theory of evolution. So it's clear to anyone reading his book that even mankind evolved from animal life and can't have any claim to be a special creation of a divine being. Of course, this caused tremendous outrage with the church at that time. The church had fervently believed that mankind was the crown of creation and that God had created man "to make the earth subservient to him."[70] Today, molecular genetics has confirmed that mankind and chimpanzees have a common ancestor: Ninety-nine percent of their genomes are identical.[71] Moreover, human genes are encoded precisely the same as with most living things on earth.[72] The few different genetic codes that also exist, as in yeast,[73] are best explained by assuming that nature always seeks new avenues into forming life.

Nonetheless, some groups of people surface every now and then like the *creationists* who truly believe that God had created every species individually, one at a time. Supporters of the so-called *Intelligent Design*, a pseudo-scientific version of creationism, think that some living things are too complex to have developed from natural selection. They also believe that the enormous increase in variety of species 540 million years ago can be explained only with the intervention from a divine source—an "intelligent designer."[74]

The fact is, life on earth excels at producing a very great variety of species. How could this come about? Essentially, in addition to Darwin's theory of evolution and Intelligent Design, there is even a third answer. So let's compare all of these and see how everything stacks up. 1) Darwin's theory of evolution states that life produces new species again and

Fourth Challenge: Chicken and Egg

again on itself, that is, *by chance* according to our third challenge. Species must then prove themselves during a process of natural selection in order to survive. The evolution of life doesn't need any God who plans, nor does it need an intelligent designer. But this theory runs into trouble because the estimated age of four billion years of life on our planet isn't really sufficient to produce its various complex forms of life. 2) Intelligent Design maintains that all of life is "designed." Some designer established a well-defined *order* by which the great variety of species would have to be created. However, this line of thinking runs into trouble, too, because it can't explain deviations from the genetic code, as in yeast, which most likely occurred by chance and not by design. Also, the designer could have spared his creation if he knew the outcome beforehand. 3) There's a third answer for the variety of species, and we already found it in our third challenge: Life is based on a very creative mix of both *order and chance*.

Let's take a closer look at the third answer and focus on the most typical feature of life: reproduction. Reproduction is the very heart of life where order and chance go hand in hand. The mechanisms of reproduction can be manifold, but they are all governed by rules. When rules are active, *order* is at work. On the other hand, it's common scientific belief that new biological species evolve from small mutations during reproduction, that is to say, from deviations of order. A new species spontaneously springs to life—there is no half-way point. So, here we have *chance* at work. I really can't think of any scientific observation that would interfere with the third answer. This answer can even tell us how the great variety of species on our planet has come about: by both order and chance. The first living cell and every new species came into being by chance. But the conditions on earth that enabled a great variety of species *don't happen* by chance, but by a consequence of natural laws that are well-suited for life. Our earth has—due to cosmically caused, unpredictable events— a distance to the sun that gives us moderate temperatures; our earth also provides plenty of water and all other elements necessary for life. Can't we see Mother Nature herself at work here? Isn't it *natural* that nature fashioned natural laws? This creative mix of both order and chance makes life worth living (figure 28).

Fig. 28: Life is a creative mix of order and chance

Today, Darwin's theory of evolution has been accepted by scientists worldwide. So, it is a great mystery to me that most of us still believe in every human being's individuality while being aware of Darwin's great revelation that no species was created individually. Let me be more specific: There aren't any individual species on earth because they all have

Fourth Challenge: Chicken and Egg

evolved from a common ancestor; so, why should mankind consist of "individuals"? The Latin word *individuum* literally means "inseparable." It represents the smallest element of a group that is indivisible and stands alone from all the other elements. It's certainly true that we are the smallest elements of humanity, but do we also stand alone from each other? This might be true physically, but genetically we are linked to one another; and all that we feel, think, and do is deeply influenced by the world around us and—more profoundly than we can ever imagine—by others!

I can be even more specific to those of us who believe in God: Why would God choose to create jointly evolving species on the one hand, but human individuals on the other? Darwin teaches us that life is *one big picture,* yet our current foreign policies in North America and Europe interfere with the evolution of life by rejecting immigrants and by impeding the mixing of genes—life prospers through mating! How could humankind survive if it is fighting against itself? And yet, most people seek individuality, and they do so for various reasons: Some of us wish to live in alleged individual freedom; others hope to preserve their alleged individuality even beyond their life on earth. Nature is pursuing a different goal: Whoever reads her clues will be deeply compelled to surrender the desire for individuality and live a far greater adventure—cosmic consciousness.

Unfortunately for nature, Darwin's theory of evolution has often been misinterpreted as a "survival of the fittest." Some dictators even justify their brutality by referring to it. But natural selection isn't at all about showing strength. To survive as a species we must learn to live in harmony with

Mother Nature. Whoever is better in adapting will have the chance to hand down his/her genes. This includes that living things eat other living things. But killing in the animal kingdom never arises from hatred[75]—animals do so only to promote the survival of their own species. In order to unfold, nature makes use of herself.

Chicken and Egg Are Not Two

According to Darwin's theory of evolution, every species on earth has gradually evolved from one (or a few) first living cell(s). And according to our third challenge, these very first cells sprang to life by chance. So we would indeed do nature a great wrong if we spoke of "the chicken" and "the egg." In fact, chickens and eggs never stopped evolving; that's why we must conceive them as one (one process). But whenever we say that chicken and egg are one, we could still think of this one process as consisting of parts—chickens and eggs. Eastern philosophers like Adi Shankara of India (ninth century AD) never spoke of "one," but of "not two."[76] Here is why: Whenever we say that chicken and egg are not two, it's clear to everyone that we *must not* view chicken and egg as two parts of one thing. As a matter of fact, chicken and egg have never been two.

I kindly invite you to read the last paragraph once more because it holds the very secret of our philosophical journey: We often think of things as being two or more although they are only one. We already discussed several examples: space

Fourth Challenge: Chicken and Egg

and time, being and becoming, good and evil. There is even more in the chapters ahead. To make things easier for you, I have always been speaking of "two sides of the same coin." This image is very familiar to us: Every coin has a front side (often showing the value of the coin) and a back side (often showing an image), but front and back sides always belong to one and the same coin. We can't separate the coin's front from the coin's back. Even if the two sides of a coin seem to be completely different at times, they can never stand alone; they are inseparably linked to each other.

So what? Well, I already told you that Plutarch's riddle isn't only about chickens and eggs. The riddle addresses the relation of parent and child, and in the most general sense, it addresses the relation of cause and effect. That is to say: The chicken also stands for my dear parents; the egg stands for my sisters and me. Another way of reading it: The chicken stands for my dear wife and me; the egg stands for our dear sons. But since chicken and egg are not two, we all (that is, my parents, my sisters, my wife and me, our sons) are also not two and not many, but just one.

Let's make the circle bigger and bigger: All of humanity are not two—all living things on earth are not two—all that there is in the universe is not two. Now we understand how powerful the concept of *not two* really is. Eastern philosophy has coined a very special term for it: *advaita* (pronounced as "a-dvaita"). The root word *dvaita* (English: duality or "two-ness") is Sanskrit and means that something can be split into two or more parts. Adding the extra syllable "a" to the word *dvaita* tells us that we're dealing with a non-duality here that can't be split into parts.

All there is in the universe is not two, but one. That is: Whenever we see two or more living things fighting against each other, it's one and the same thing fighting against itself. Two roosters fighting for a hen—they're one. A fox killing a lamb—they're one. Mankind fighting against itself—they're one. Now for the first time, we are prompted to reflect more deeply on ourselves: Plutarch's riddle applies to you and me as well! Its most significant implication for mankind is that you and I are also not two, but one.

Who or what am I? This is a very tricky question for us to solve because it contains a hidden reference to itself—like the concept of "all-powerful." The "I" in "Who or what am I?" is self-defeating. However, unlike "all-powerful" that we unmasked as a void concept, there should be an answer to the question about ourselves. Several brilliant philosophers have already racked their brains to come up with an answer. French philosopher René Descartes linked the "I" to *thought*: "I think, therefore I am."[77] His conclusion seems very logical at first glance, but it turns out to be a vicious cycle: The assumption "I think" already implies that my "I" exists; from this assumption, we must not deduce that I am.

German philosopher Ludwig Feuerbach abandoned the idea of deducing the "I" from thought. He embraced *feeling*: "I feel, therefore I am."[78] Feuerbach considered feeling the very essence of being. The "I" is an "affair of the heart," and thought is an "affair of the head."[79] The idea of highlighting feeling was great, but Feuerbach walked right into the same trap as Descartes did: The assumption "I feel" already implies that my "I" exists; from this assumption, we must not deduce that I am.

Fourth Challenge: Chicken and Egg

French poet Arthur Rimbaud was clever enough to turn the tables: "It's thinking me."[80] We might even want to add feeling: It's thinking *and feeling* me. It was a very smart move to convert the subject "I" into the object "me" because this concept shifts our focus away from the "I" towards a verb. Whoever is engaged in meditation does the same thing. He or she focuses on an activity to let oneself go: "It's *breathing* me." According to Rimbaud, I am a thought—and perhaps a feeling. Of course, one question remains: When we choose to say "it's thinking me," then who is the "it"? We could set the "it" equal to a wildcard (God or an "intelligent designer"), but then we would have merely replaced our original question "Who or what am I?" with "Who or what is it?"

There is another answer to "Who or what am I?" that is far more compelling than everything that we have discussed so far. David Hume, economist and philosopher from Scotland, brought it up, but didn't draw the right conclusion. He claimed that the "I" is a succession of sensory impressions; there is nothing continual that could match a sovereign and static "I."[81] This idea laid the groundwork for today's view of the "I," but Hume didn't finish the job himself: If the "I" can't be static, it must be *dynamic*—a process! A sixty-year-old man isn't the same anymore as he was when he was ten. At the age of sixty, he certainly has different feelings, different thoughts, and even a different body! Almost all of our cells are replaced every few years without our even noticing a thing.[82] I never am, yet I *become* all of my life. So, the concept of a personal self that comes with its own identity and that is solely responsible for all of its actions—this concept is valid only under human jurisdiction.

The strongest evidence for a dynamic "I" is provided by quantum physics and is less than a hundred years old. Since then, the "I" has rocketed to a shooting star within physics: The "I" stands for "observing"! Quantum theory isn't just a pipe dream of physics because it has provided us with many technical achievements such as television, computers, lasers, and nuclear power plants. So, insights from quantum theory can't be all wrong. Its key message guides us: There are no passive objects in the cosmos; everything is *interacting* with its environment. So, that's why verbs ("human becoming," "chicken-ing," "egg-ing") describe reality more adequately than nouns. Detached spectators—as in classical physics—don't exist anymore. Everything is linked to everything else. The cosmos and every living thing that it embraces are an inseparable, continually unfolding *process*.

Werner Heisenberg,
German physicist
(1901 – 1976)

German physicist Werner Heisenberg enjoyed teaching a little thought experiment to illustrate the inseparable unity of an observer and the observed. It is sketched in figure 29. The goal is to find the exact position of a particle. To achieve this, Heisenberg places it under a microscope. He also turns on a lamp so that he can see the particle. But now, the light transfers some energy onto the particle and unintentionally puts it into motion. So, the mere attempt to observe the particle compels it to move and continually change its position. Of course, the opposite effect takes place too: Observing the moving particle continually changes things in Heisenberg's brain; nerves are stimulated and new cellular links emerge while the observation is being stored in his mind.

Fig. 29: Trying to find the exact position of a particle (red)

Let's finish our fourth challenge with another example that demonstrates how dynamic the "I" is. What do you see in figure 30: berries, vegetables, grains, or nuts? Please have a look at the figure first, then make a guess, and finally look up the solution in the chapter entitled *Notes*.[83]

Fig. 30: Berries, vegetables, grains, or nuts?

Well? Did you know the answer beforehand, or are you surprised now? If you made a wrong guess as most people do, then you have just learned what the strawberry really is. If you made the right guess, I still have a nice surprise saved up for you: If you ever consume a luscious piece of strawberry shortcake again, then you'll know from now on that it isn't a berry cake, but a . . . cake! And here's my point: A few minutes ago, you didn't know the truth about strawberries or strawberry shortcakes yet. Don't you agree that you are somehow different now than what you were before?

So, I'm not a who, but a process, a verb form, a "human becoming." In more tangible words: I become through every experience that my body has. Yet since we're all interacting with each other, there's no "individual myself" and no "individual yourself." There's only a "cosmic ourselves"—the sum of all experiencing in the cosmos. It's precisely this ourselves that we should cherish and embrace instead of clinging to an illusionary individuality.

Message of our fourth challenge:
There is no chicken without egg,
and no egg without chicken.

Alternative ways to express this message:
Chicken and egg are not two.
Chicken and egg are two sides of the same coin.

The coin's name is: living.

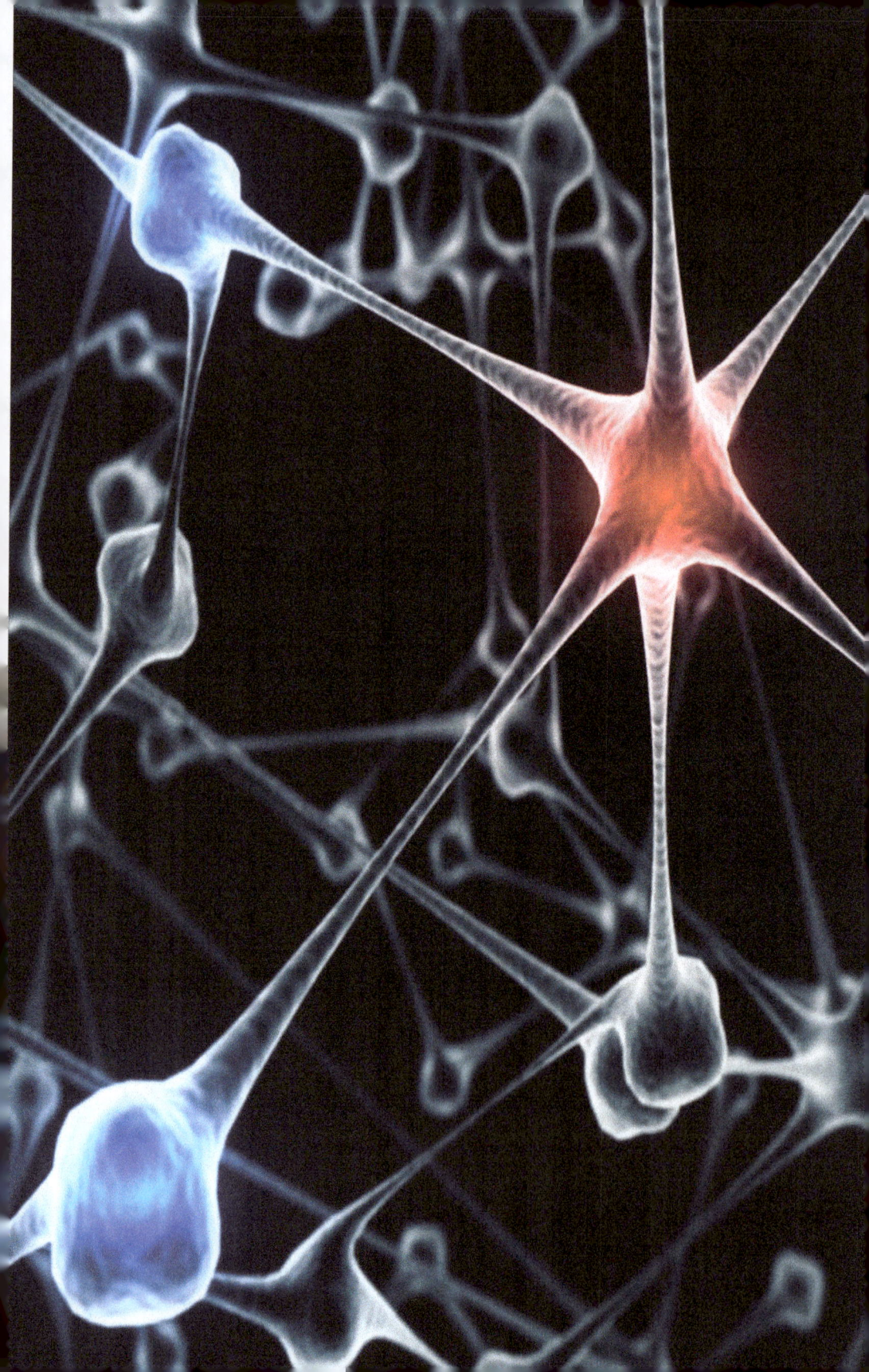

Fifth Challenge: Creator and Creation

Fifth Challenge: Creator and Creation

Which Comes First—Creator or Creation?

> A COSMOS IN WHICH LIFE JUST HAPPENS
> IS AS CREATIVE AS ANY GOD CAN BE.

Here we are! You will soon hold the solution to the deepest puzzle ever *in your very hands*. You can bet that I won't give you the answer on a silver platter. I want you to find it for yourself; after having solved the previous challenge, you'll get the idea quickly. There is, of course, a good reason why I'm not giving you the answer right away: *learning by doing*. Whatever you do on your own you will never forget all of your life.

You have already learned that neither chicken nor egg came first because they are causing one another. Here comes your challenge:

Replace "the chicken" with "creator."
Replace "the egg" with "creation."

Our question "Which comes first—the chicken or the egg?" then turns into: "Which comes first—creator or creation?"

Now transfer all that you've learned about chicken and egg to our new terms "creator" and "creation."

Please close your book while doing so.
Good luck!

Which Comes First — Creator or Creation?

If you followed my instructions one by one, then I can tell that you just had a spiritual experience. You recognized something surprising and very extraordinary: Even creator and creation can cause one another. Just as a chicken lays an egg and a *slightly different chicken* emerges, a creator can also "lay" a creation and a *slightly different creator* "emerges." But how can we actually tell that creator and creation are causing one another like chicken and egg? Well, the Romanesco broccoli displayed in figure 31 left gives it all away: Nature just loves creating *fractals*—structures that look roughly the same on different scales.

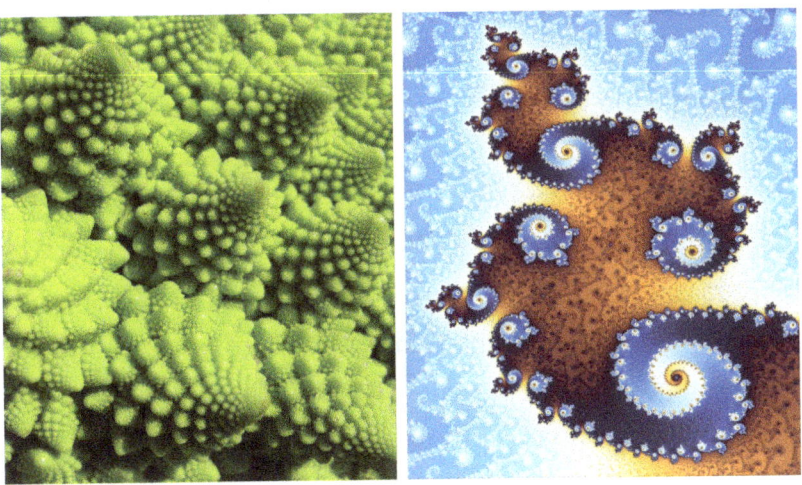

Fig. 31: Fractals in nature and mathematics

Figure 31 right illustrates another self-similar structure, yet it comes from a mathematical process: a *recursive* formula that tells us how an element z_n of a sequence generates the next element z_{n+1}. Romanesco as well as chicken and egg are

Fifth Challenge: Creator and Creation

examples that show how nature makes use of mathematical algorithms. Let me share another wonderful example of self-similarity with you: the biological evolution taking place on earth and the unfolding of a human embryo. In the course of three to four billion years, highly complex creatures developed on earth from unicellular organisms; in the course of nine months, a new "human becoming" develops from two nuclei in the mother's womb.

Whether we believe in a creator or not, one thing is for sure: If there is a creator, we could never fathom nor conceive even the slightest understanding of him; because if we could, it would make us superior to him. This is why Holy Scriptures are very wise when they tell us not to make any images of God. But still, two billion[84] Christians paint a very human picture of a "son of God"—and this picture is something very uncertain.

Our human communication falls woefully short in being able to accurately describe a creator of the universe. The only language that can match the precision of a God accurately and fairly is mathematics. Perhaps it's not by chance that so many events in nature unfold through recursive processes and formulas. Isn't it obvious why nature has such "fondness" for recursive processes? Well, let's face it: Nature is creator *and* creation at once! And so, we already know the answer to the question about which one comes first—neither one of them. Neither one comes first because even creator and creation are causing one another. Along with every new generation, not only the creation continues to develop, but also its creator. Yet every recursive algorithm—this includes the evolution of life—has a very first element z_1. So who or what started the evolution, that is, who or what created this very first element? Well, we already know the answer from our third challenge when we talked about order and chance: Matter is either not alive or alive. So, the transition from one to the other *must* have been spontaneous (by chance), which tells us that it had no cause at all.

Moses' Genesis

In ancient times, people had entirely different points of view about a creator. One concept that has held on until the present day goes all the way back to a famous prophet who was supposed to have rescued the people of Israel from Egyptian slavery—Moses.

Moses,
Jewish prophet
(perhaps a myth)

The *Old Testament* starts with the *Five Books of Moses*. We don't know whether Moses lived at all, but scientists today agree that he was not the author of these five books.[85] Even so, the first of these books, the **Genesis**, still carries his name: *The First Book of Moses*. It describes the creation of the world: "In the beginning, God created the heavens and the earth. And the earth was waste and void; and darkness was upon the face of the deep: and the Spirit of God moved upon the face of the waters. And God said, let there be light: and there was light. And God saw the light, that it was good: and God divided the light from the darkness. God called the light *day*, and the darkness he called *night*. And there was evening and there was morning, one day."[86] And so, God was supposed to have created the world in in seven days.

Day 1: Creation of light (day and night)
Day 2: Creation of the heavens
Day 3: Separation of land from water, creation of plants
Day 4: Creation of heavenly bodies
Day 5: Creation of marine creatures and birds
Day 6: Creation of land animals and humankind
Day 7: On the Sabbath, God finishes his work and rests

The biblical chronology that describes the creation of all structures and living things corresponds astoundingly well with the findings of modern science. A period of only seven days for the creation of our world, of course, falls much too short, especially when we consider that the period of time for a human embryo to mature takes as long as nine months. More than 2,000 years ago, there was a good reason why the authors of *Genesis* envisioned a creation of the world within *days:* Back then, people still lived from day to day; a stretch of time such as four billion years was yet unknown.

In contrast, Figure 32 shows a time scale of how life on earth has developed according to the scientific knowledge that we have today. During a *physical* and a *chemical* evolution on earth, about a billion years went by until the first unicellular organisms emerged from hydrocarbons, ammonia, and water. Another 2.6 billion years later, these organisms suddenly merged together to form multicellular organisms, allowing them to accomplish far more than before through task-sharing. As time went on, random jumps occurred time and again: transfer of life from water onto land, photosynthesis, formation of bones, creation of mammals, walking upright. Every jump gave the species that were involved an *advantage* over all of the other species. This *biological evolution* (evolution of the species) was investigated by Charles Darwin. Finally and somewhat delayed in time, the *spiritual evolution* (evolution of consciousness) is happening.[87] Consciousness is the capability to spiritually conceive and process a perception that has occurred materially. Fish were probably the first living things equipped with a consciousness.

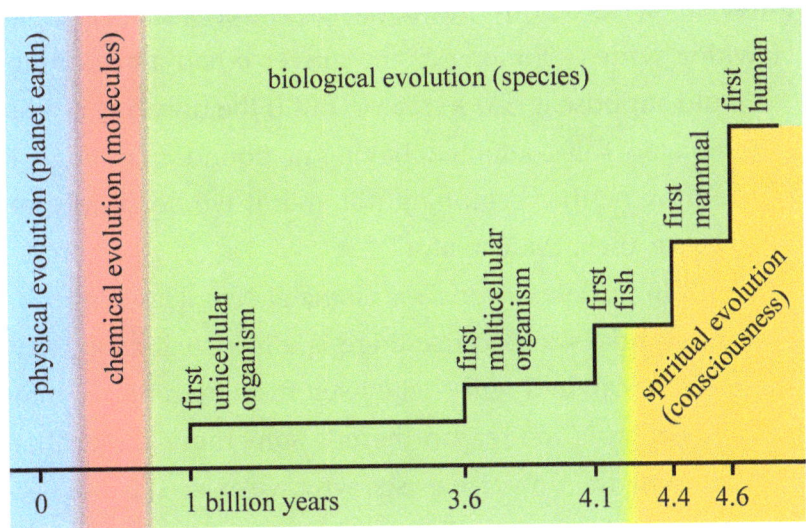

Fig. 32: History of evolution on earth

Fifth Challenge: Creator and Creation

Hawking's Universe

British physicist Stephen Hawking became famous for his work with *black holes*. Black holes are objects that have such a strong gravitational force around them that all energy, all mass, and even all information are trapped within them. But Hawking's lifelong work was also dedicated to the history of the universe.

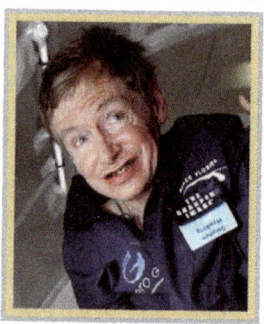

Stephen Hawking,
British physicist
(1942 – 2018)

There's definitely no room for a creator in Hawking's **universe.** In his world-wide bestseller *A Brief History of Time*, Hawking writes: "So long as the universe had a beginning, we could suppose it had a creator. But if the universe is really completely self-contained, having no boundary or edge, it would have neither beginning nor end: it would simply be. What place, then, for a creator?"[88]

And in his latest work *The Grand Design*, Hawking gets even more precise: "Because there is a law such as gravity, the universe can and will create itself from nothing. Spontaneous creation is the reason there is something rather than nothing, why the universe exists, why we exist. It is not necessary to invoke God to light the blue touch paper and set the universe going."[89]

These statements also make very clear how narrow the concepts of "creator" and "God" actually were to Hawking. Unlike Albert Einstein, who viewed God very abstractly as the causal forces of nature, Hawking always associated the concepts of "creator" and "God" with a person. It was out of the question for Hawking that a creator—in case one were to unexpectedly exist—would have to reside somewhere outside of the universe. Hawking's question "What place, then, for a creator?" demonstrates that even the thought of a creator dwelling within his own creation was completely foreign to him.

So, has the existence of a creator now become obsolete to modern physics? No way! But we have to emphasize that the question about a creator has never been—and never will be—a matter for physics because physics describes nature and doesn't challenge it. Yet Stephen Hawking stands for an attitude that had already been addressed in a study in 1998 and published in the scientific journal *Nature:* At the beginning of the twentieth century, 35 percent of all leading scientists believed in a personal God and their own immortality; toward the end of that century, this number dropped down to only 7 percent.[90] Apparently, the tremendous strides of knowledge in the field of physics led to a significant change with regard to religious beliefs. Many physicists still believe in God or a creator—but no longer hold fast in their belief in a personal one.[91] However, one thing is for sure: Physicists will never stop believing. They have to believe in their own theories because they can never prove them. Any scientific theory must include the possibility of it being disproved—for example, by performing an experiment.

Whitehead's Organism

Alfred North Whitehead—what a name! It's as if his parents already knew that their son would someday show humanity the way: north, and in a special sense "the way upward." To this day, Whitehead's world view is virtually unknown to most of us, yet no one seems to have come any closer to the truth about life and God than he has. At the age of eighteen, Whitehead took up mathematics as his major area of study. In his main work, *Process and Reality*,[92] he put together all of his insights after years of meditation.

Alfred North Whitehead, *British mathematician and philosopher* (1861 – 1947)

Whitehead is probably the most important pioneer of metaphysics of the twentieth century. Yet most of us only know his name and his claim that Western philosophy is nothing more than a "series of footnotes" to Plato.[93] But by doing so, he only wanted to affirm that today no philosopher can escape Plato's way of thinking anymore—not even in the slightest way. Whitehead developed a speculative, but very powerful theory that is a philosophy of life and a world view in one. His central idea is straightforward: A creative power dwells throughout the cosmos, and life is an expression of this creative power.

Even if Whitehead's texts are difficult reading, his theory truly stands out because it is remarkably consistent with modern physics. Like quantum physics, Whitehead considers the cosmos to be a process. This is why we will now take a detailed look at his ideas.

Whitehead's theory has been given the name "process philosophy," but this label disguises its most important attribute: vitality. Whitehead himself speaks of a *philosophy of organism*.[94] And indeed, he conceives the unique qualities of an **organism**—experiences—as the cornerstones of the cosmos. Whitehead does not call them elementary particles, but *drops of experience*.[95] "Objects" like human beings (actually: "human becomings"), animals, plants, sand, or atoms would not exist in themselves. In fact, verbs would create and form the things that we call "objects." Everything in the universe would be relational. That is to say: Everything would exist only as a feeling of connection to everything else. So, even every electron can feel: By "feeling" an electromagnetic field within the very same atom that it belongs to, the electron is guided around its orbit. It is "feeling" that transforms it into an electron.

According to Whitehead, there is no dead matter; everything is reacting to something else in some kind of way. Everything in the universe would be permeated and actuated by *creative energy*.[96] Whitehead turns directly against his French colleague René Descartes who presented a dualistic world view—consciousness on the one hand, dead matter on the other. According to Whitehead, the world does not split into parts. Cosmos would be *alive* and embody itself in everything that lives (figure 33).

Fifth Challenge: Creator and Creation

Fig. 33: Indian summer

Philosophy enables us to compare different views of the world, to revise them, to expand them, or—if necessary—to reject them. As a philosopher, Whitehead is pursuing particularly one goal: He wants to understand what experiences are. After all, we all have experiences throughout our lives. Whitehead emphasizes how important it is to face our experiences and to learn from them; only through our experience could we be happy and satisfied with our lives. But Whitehead also stresses that any assumption to know the ultimate truth would be an "exhibition of folly."[97] Reality would always be far beyond our grasp. It would live from new and surprising experiences that are generated again and again in the cosmos.

Whitehead shares such a surprising experience with us. Let me show you how it works. We are well accustomed to consider subjects as primal and to subordinate predicates: *I read.* Here, we quietly accept that the "I" has its own existence and can "do" and "experience" just about everything. But reality is different according to Whitehead: Our nouns wouldn't come close to describing reality. Everything would start from "experiencing," but it's not the "I" that has experiences, but the process of experiencing makes an "I" from matter.[98] And this is precisely why Whitehead calls his theory *philosophy of organism* and why he stresses "organism" to be one thing—singular. He truly conceives all of reality as one living organism, an unfolding "not-two"; and we are its experiences. The cosmos and "I" are not two—we are one. So, Whitehead is a radical empiricist, and we can learn very much from his thoughts and ideas—above all a deeply ecological view of nature that gives us a unique and precious, but also very fragile living sphere.

Whitehead says that reality isn't made up of objects, but of processes of becoming. So we can now appreciate the title of his work: *Process and Reality*. Becoming occurs in specific patterns: *order and novelty*.[99] Order stems from mathematics; it reveals itself in all laws of nature. Whitehead's concept of *novelty* is revolutionary because it breathes life and energy into his theory. Indeed, most philosophers consider lifeless facts to be the ultimate of the world. But Whitehead strongly disagrees: Processes are the ultimate. The cosmos would not consist *of* objects, but *through its involvement with* objects that mutually rearrange themselves and thereby bring out surprising turns in nature. Whitehead personally likes to speak of *accidents*.[100] According to him, these accidents can be joyful and absolutely overwhelming.

Whitehead has a unique name for the primal activity that everything comes from: *creativity*.[101] Not only mankind is creative, but nature herself would produce unfathomable creativity. And indeed, this hypothesis is supported today in many ways: Snow crystals, eyes of insects, and honeycomb cells—they all decree a six-sided symmetry that makes the most of existing space (figure 34). On the other hand, ferns, snail shells, and spiral galaxies all develop into a spiral form that gives them specific stability within the physical world (figure 35). Such symmetries and forms show that the laws of nature evoke *order* within the cosmos. But they also give evidence of nature's creativity as it unfolds to induce *novelty*: bees that build symmetric combs, and snails that carry stable shells on their bodies—all for the very first time and in unique perfection.

Fig. 34: Snow crystal, eye of insect, honeycomb

Fig. 35: Fern, snail shell, spiral galaxy

I also have a very human example for creativity: When our son was learning to talk, he would surprise us almost every day with funny word creations. One morning he came bouncing into our kitchen with beaming eyes as he pointed down to his pants and shouted proudly: "Butt-sweater!" We can all chuckle about it today, but at the time when he was discovering verbal language for himself, such words were like greetings from a distant star—as if creativity were the most natural thing of the world.

Whitehead defines eight *categories of existence*,[102] all continuously interconnected as they intertwine with each other like a Buddhistic mandala (figure 36).

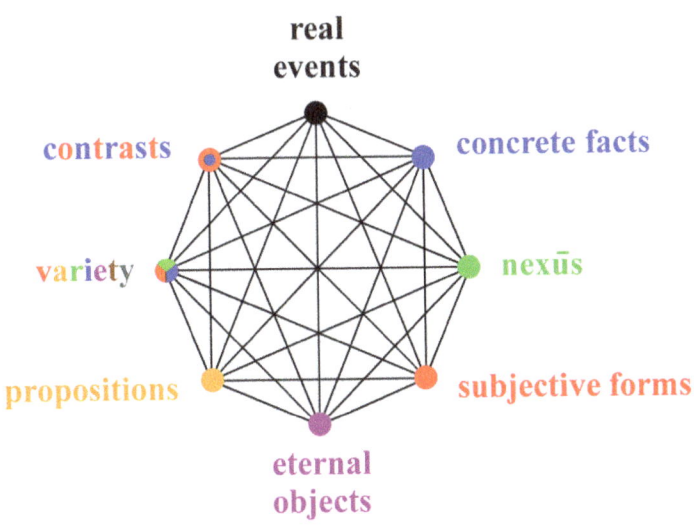

Fig. 36: Eight categories of existence according to Whitehead

Real Events are the drops of experience that I already mentioned. When an experience occurs, it becomes a part of the past, but is not lost. I have one experience after another, which means that I am a sequence of real events—drops of experience. With every subsequent experience, I become a slightly modified drop of experience, which in truth is a *new* drop of experience. And so, every experience increases its grand total in the universe by one. Since all experiences are interconnected, they are all "in me"—people and things that produced me, taught me, and shaped me. That's why no one is solely responsible for what he/she does! We always bear responsibility together.

Concrete Facts are everything that we experience and that moves us. According to Whitehead, they include a distinct direction, which means that they convey energy and/or information. Many concrete facts bind us to the past, and so, they belong to reality. Other concrete facts are experienced and felt, and while they are in our minds, they are not part of reality—like goals, wishes, intentions, imaginations, and abstract ideas.[103]

Nexūs are linked events. Cells that form an organism and trees that make a forest are just two examples. Nexūs with social orders make *societies*.[104] Societies have a greater stability, and they can consist of societies too. For instance, our planet earth is a society consisting of societies consisting of societies ... According to Whitehead, all reality is permeated by social order.

Subjective Forms are feelings, valuations, inclinations, dislikes, and also awareness. They are all subjective because they all shape us. Subjective forms convey essentially who I am. In any given moment, I am nothing more than what I feel and how I value something. During this experience, my

"I" is slightly changing. Do you remember what Heraclitus once said? No one ever steps into the same river twice. We discussed two interpretations. Whitehead likes the second one best: According to Whitehead, you will never have the same experience twice because you are no longer the same after an experience. The "I" can never be a constant thing as it is one drop of experience after another.

Figure 37 summarizes what we've just learned: In every moment I am a drop of experience—in transition from a past that has just been concluded into a wide-open future that is about to be now. The past consists of concrete facts and other events that might be linked to each other as nexūs. All of the things that I felt and valued in one moment of the past (marked in grey) are subjective forms. Just one moment later (marked in black), I am a new drop of experience that has changed ever-so-slightly—and the universe is all-the-more precious because of it.

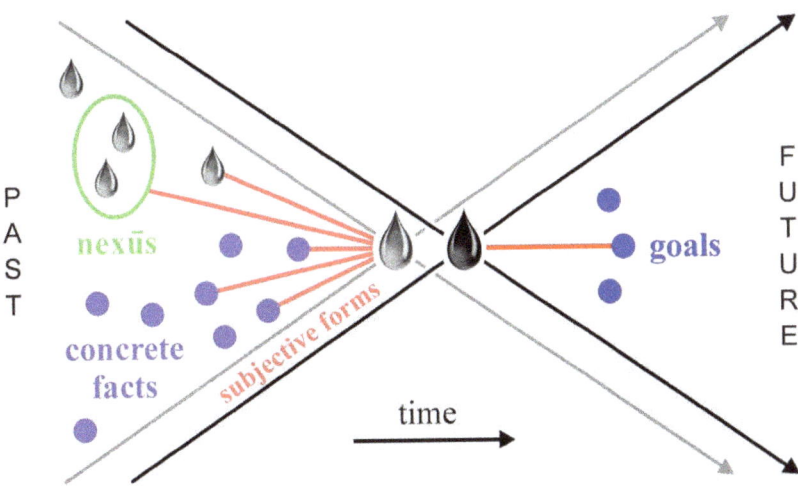

Fig. 37: Concrete facts, nexūs, and subjective forms

Eternal Objects—when Whitehead talks about objects, he doesn't mean material objects, but objects that exist independent of time. The concept "eternal" stands for something that can always be replicated. Colors are a good example: The shade of violet can always be recalled from experience as long as the physical requirements for its realization are given. The sky can have various colors like blue, red, or violet. The color that we might see at any given time depends on several factors including the time of day. But if the sky above us appears blue at noon, the color of violet still exists and hasn't perished or disappeared from the universe; it can always be reproduced as an experience again, for example just after sunset. In this way, Whitehead shows very clearly the difference between *possibility* and *reality*.

Other examples for eternal objects are geometric shapes and numbers (figure 38). Eternal objects are different from real events because they neither have feelings nor do they make decisions; so, they can't be creative in any way. Eternal objects and real events, however, are the only categories with final character. This is why I have put them in figure 36 into two distinct regions: eternal objects at the bottom and real events at the top.

Fig. 38: Examples of eternal objects

Propositions are our vital sources of novelty—for that which is new. Whitehead also calls them *lures for feeling*.[105] Examples of propositions are inspirations that guide a musician while in the act of improvising or the many charms and impulses that cause us to laugh at a good joke. Propositions motivate us to make spontaneous choices; and they encourage us to take steps into new directions. They are what bring a breath of fresh air into our lives.

Variety gives reality its warmth and charm. How unbearably monotonous the cosmos would be without it! With variety's magic and splendor, God finally enters into Whitehead's world view: God created all of the many possibilities and therefore knows what the future holds. But what turns out to become real is decided by life—some possibilities are chosen, others are not. Even God wouldn't know in advance what will be decided; Whitehead also considers the will to be free! To keep all of our options open, we would be well-advised to promote variety on earth: ecologically, culturally, religiously. By the way, the splendor of variety is bound into distance: Spatial distance enables us *to be different*; temporal distance enables us *to become different*.

Contrasts are only possible if there is variety. Contrasts exist in many ways as colors, forms, sounds, feelings, and relationships. They do not necessarily lead to conflicts, but they gently stress differences. Whitehead says that contrasts help us know where we can strive and find greatest value in life: beauty and harmony. Just one mindful glance into the brilliance of nature (figure 39 left) or just one harmonious cadence of music (figure 39 right) will do, and we will never be able to break its spell—ever again.

Fifth Challenge: Creator and Creation

Fig. 39: Contrasts enable beauty and harmony

There are many sources of harmony: art, music, ethics, religion, and science. We can profit from all of them equally, but many people limit themselves and think that either their own religion or science is uniquely privileged. According to Whitehead, we can put harmony not only into words and formulas, but we can also dance it or paint it. Whitehead shows us how a world view can be comprehensive and conclusive in one—he gives us beautiful instructions that help us to understand the world. It is his vivid approach to life which makes Whitehead all the more likeable.

My love of harmony motivated me to write this book and assign Alfred North Whitehead a central role in it. In an age where mankind is destroying the ecological splendor of the earth a million times faster than it takes to create it, in which we use terror and destruction to grind cultural monuments into the earth, in which we use our religious faiths to fight one another—in such a time there is NOTHING more important nor more vital than to foster a society that is creative, compassionate, respectful, and that has the ecological wisdom to never exclude *any* living thing that is among us from this society. We owe this not only to a God, but especially to ourselves.

In my search for the meaning of life, I have never been able to find any greater treasure than the treasure of Alfred North Whitehead. His concept of God is one of such striking beauty and loving-inclusiveness that it would be difficult to embrace any other God—once you have read and conceived the following lines:

> "It is as true to say
> that God is one and the World many,
> as that the World is one and God many;
>
> ... that, in comparison with the World, God is actual eminently,
> as that, in comparison with God, the World is actual eminently;
>
> ... that the World is immanent in God,
> as that God is immanent in the World;
>
> ... that God transcends the World,
> as that the World transcends God;
>
> ... (and) that God creates the World,
> as that the World creates God."[106]

Nothing can be added to these words by Whitehead. It is a poem about a great philosopher's love for God. Perhaps you must read it ten times, as I have, before the greatness of this treasure finally dawned upon me as I hope it will also dawn upon you: Whitehead teaches us how to love a God that truly is a God of every living thing.

Creator and Creation Are Not Two

You can probably guess where our fifth challenge is going: Since creator and creation mutually depend on each other, it is very clear to see that they are not separate—not two. And through it all, this conclusion is far more significant than all of the others put together. This time, it's about something very intimate that believers call "God."

Many people don't even want to get into the subject of "God" because it is beset with so many antiquated and contradictory ideas. One of them—the all-powerful God—has previously been unmasked as a logical impossibility. We can live peacefully with one another if we thoroughly question concepts about God that have been obsolete for a very long time, and if we follow Whitehead by taking steps into new directions. The same goes for Christianity. I repeat my saying from the introduction: "When you wish to find a clue, try to change your point of view!" Of course, this advice also applies to our search for God. We limit our search area far too drastically whenever we reduce the idea of "God" to a person only.

Our chapter *Leibniz' Theodicy* concluded with the words: "God can't intervene into our world because God isn't outside of our world." And at long last, after wrestling with this challenge, we found out where our connection with God is: in the midst of its creation, that is, *within* our world. God is far more than just a creator—God is also its entire creation. I believe like Whitehead that we meet God in everything that lives: in every plant, in every animal, and in everyone of us. We live with God as one (figure 40).

Creator and Creation Are Not Two

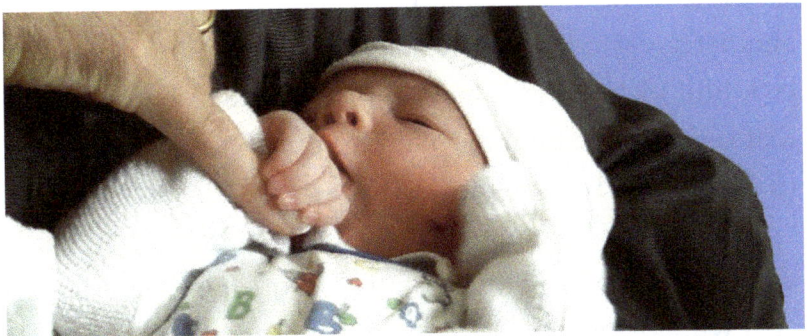

Fig. 40: We meet God in everything that lives

So, Whitehead's view of the world truly makes sense. The entire cosmos is *one living organism*. And this is precisely why I now propose to us—and to all of humanity—the following: Let's put all of our images and pre-conceived ideas about the existence of God aside! Whitehead identified creativity as the primal activity that everything comes from. So, let's simply view God as *creativity*—the same creativity that has created everything as the one that is at work in us when we live, love, paint, make music, write books, or create new words like "butt-sweater." And then, world peace will take a great leap forward since no one can ever doubt that such a creativity—such a God—truly exists.

If we make this conception of God part of us and honor *all creativity* within the cosmos (of course, this implies that we mutually respect each other, that we always live mindfully, and that we cherish all of nature's outstanding creativity), then we will finally regain what humankind actually stands for: humanity.

Fifth Challenge: Creator and Creation

We can now add to our collection of "not-two" concepts another great non-duality: creator and creation. There is a beautiful picture that comes to us from Chinese philosophy that captures the fundamental idea of *not two*: Yin and Yang (figure 41). In Taoism, the dark Yin stands for "smooth" and "peaceful" and "feminine"; the light Yang stands for "hard" and "in motion" and "masculine." Frequently, Yin is associated with loving while Yang is associated with knowing. Yin and Yang flow into each other and—by doing so—they generate something completely new and unique.

Fig. 41: Yin and Yang

Yet Yin and Yang also symbolize creator (Yin) and creation (Yang); together they are God. The thing that fascinates me the most is how they mutually go hand in hand. That is to say: Such a God can create itself. Just for comparison: The creator-god for our modern day religions (Christianity, Islam, and Judaism) can't solve one very important question. Who created God? These religions can't explain the origin of God. Only a God that is creator and creation all at once can create itself. This one argument alone should give pause for thought for anyone who attempts to reduce God to a single creator; especially since we find the Yin-Yang concept in full swing throughout all of nature. Just compare figures 23 and 41—even chicken and egg pave the way for each other!

Conceiving God as both creator and creation implies an unfolding God. That's why I suggest coining the word "god-ing" like "human becoming," "chicken-ing," "egg-ing." Our noun "God" stands for creator and creation. The verb form "god-ing" emphasizes activity: unfolding, being creative. Of course, it will take us time to get used to an unfolding God. But shouldn't God be free to feel and to learn, too? Feel and learn through all living things? Through us? This concept of God might sound revolutionary, but it isn't. It is practiced in the mystical traditions of all world religions.[107]

At the end of this challenge, I cordially invite you to think about an analogy: Are there painters without paintings? Or are there paintings without painters? The answer is "no" to both questions. It's the same with creator and creation: Creator and creation are a twinpack. It's for this reason that creator and creation are not two.

Message of our fifth challenge:
*There is no creator without creation,
and no creation without creator.*

Alternative ways to express this message:
*Creator and creation are not two.
Creator and creation are two sides of the same coin.*

The coin's name is: *God.*

Sixth Challenge:
Love and Understanding

Sixth Challenge: Love and Understanding

Which Comes First—Love or Understanding?

>MANY PATHS
>LEAD TO THE TRUTH.
>
>THE EASIEST IS RELIGION.
>THE SHORTEST IS SCIENCE.
>THE MOST INSPIRING IS PHILOSOPHY.
>
>BUT THE MOST PEACEFUL ARE THESE THREE:
>MATHEMATICS, ART, AND MUSIC.

We use mainly two sources to get to the truth of the cosmos: religion (which means "binding back to something before") and science. At first glance, you might think that two things couldn't be more different. Religion approaches things *dogmatically:* Its foundation is faith; this faith relies upon texts that have survived and are no longer challenged. Science, on the other hand, is *pragmatic* and very adaptive: Its foundation is verifiable facts; scientific theories are always adjusted according to the latest observations, and they explicitly require critical scrutiny.

It actually appears as if the two paths that lead to the truth of the cosmos diverge so drastically that they would never be able to lead us to the same destination (figure 42). Yet again and again we should bring to our minds that both religion and science deal with our very same world, and so, it must be the same destination.

Which Comes First—Love or Understanding?

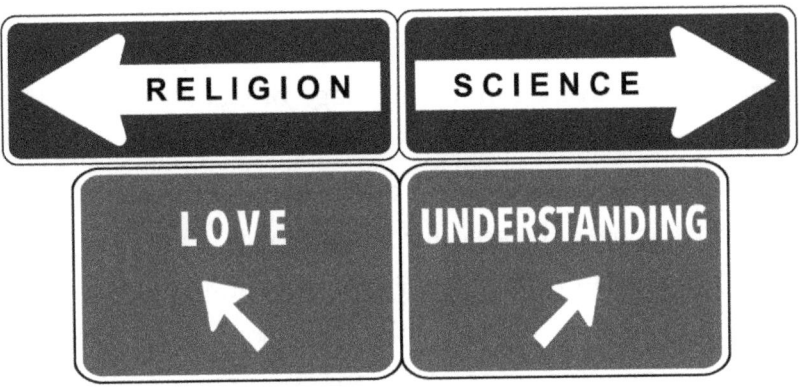

Fig. 42: Where are religion and science taking us?

Some time ago, German mystic Willigis Jaeger taught me an extremely wise point of view: Religion, science, and Buddhism are signposts that orient us in our search for the truth. Finding the truth is our true goal. And here's what's important: Truth is never outside of us, but always among us. It can best be understood from the top of a high mountain that we can climb as we take any path that we might choose. Some of these paths are longer, others are shorter (in figure 43: **H**induism, **B**uddhism, **S**cience, **C**hristianity, **J**udaism, **Is**lam). I myself consider science to be a shortcut to the truth because it uses mathematics as a prosaic but very precise language.

The scientific path has the big advantage that it *doesn't* need any personification of the divine. And by doing so, it doesn't give rise to any hostilities. Christianity, Islam, and Judaism have common roots, but their believers are at odds with each other about the meaning of a Jesus of Nazareth. The Christians view him as the son of God, the Muslims as a prophet of God. Jewish people believe that a human being can never be divine; furthermore, in "God's son," the Christians would have a forbidden image of God. The Christian faith is actually inconsistent in this point because the Bible also states that we shouldn't make images of God.[108] A personality has been the seed for many bloody wars of religion. Jesus would roll over in his grave if he still could! Yet this conflict can be solved by thinking of "son" as an unnamed metaphor: as "egg" or as "creation." We can understand the Christian Trinity in precisely this way: God is creator ("Father"), creation ("Son"), and being creative ("Holy Ghost"). The Holy Ghost stands for "breath" or "wind"—something that breathes life into the cosmos. By the way, God sacrifices his son in the same way as nature sacrifices living things—for the evolution of life!

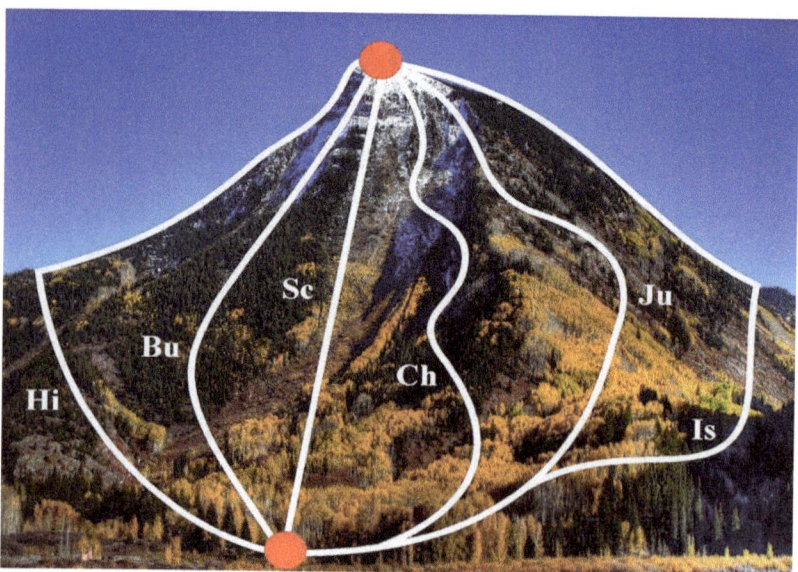

Fig. 43: Many paths lead to the truth

Using the example of light itself, I would like to illustrate how different the paths to the truth can be. The Holy Scriptures personify and glorify the light:

New Testament   "I am the light of the world.
Whoever follows me
will never walk in darkness,
but will have the light of life."[109]

Koran   "Allah is the light of the heavens and the earth.
His light is like a niche that holds a lamp.
The lamp is within glass.
The glass is like a shining star . . .
Light upon light.
God leads to his light
whomever he pleases.
And God gives parables to mankind.
And God knows everything."[110]

Old Testament   "The Lord is my light and my salvation.
Whom should I fear?"[111]

Bhagavad Gita   "He is the light of light
that banishes all darkness.
He abides in the heart of every creature,
infinitely awake within himself."[112]

Sutras   "And as he is light, so also life,
he is eternal. So he is Amida,
the fullness of everlasting life."[113]

Sixth Challenge: Love and Understanding

And what news is physics giving us about the subject of light? I had already shown that clocks go slower and rulers are shorter whenever they are moving relatively to me (see figures 7 and 9). The greater the relative speed, even greater will both effects stand out. In our challenge 2, I revealed that there is no distance within all light. That is: Within all light, each spatial and each temporal distance turns zero. So, for the light, everything is "here" and "now." That is to say: All is intimate and familiar to the light. Even without religious lyrics we see that a God, who has access to light's memory, loves us all and knows it all! God loves us all and knows it all *because*, from our perspective, God feels and learns.

Jesus Christ calls himself the "light of the world." In my opinion, this is one of the few places in the Bible that are not meant to be a parable. I believe that Jesus is expressly urging us to take him by his word, letter for letter: He is showing us the path to God, and this path leads straight into the light. It's anyone's guess whether Jesus had really lived and spoken these words. But the fact is, everything that is reported about him attests to a very wise and peaceable human being. His message was as simple as this: "Love your neighbor as yourself."[114]

And no matter how simple this message might sound, it is far more than just the trademark of the Christian faith. It rebels passionately against our unbroken desire for individuality which is the source of all conflict that is in the world today.[115] If I love someone or something intensively, something very special happens between the thing that I love and myself: The thing that I love and I become a whole. Love makes two things turn into one. And here's the kicker: The more I love something, the more familiar it becomes to me—I begin to understand it. *Understanding springs from love.* But it's also the other way around: The more I understand something, the more intimate it becomes to me—I begin to love it. *Love springs from understanding.* So, love and understanding always go hand in hand. And the answer to our question "Which comes first—love or understanding?" is once again: neither one of them.

True Love

Do you have a hobby? Anything that you really love to do? Just because it's fun? I have three such hobbies: philosophy, nature, and playing the piano. At this very moment, you are holding a product of my first hobby in your hands; I love to think about the countless facets of life and write all of my thoughts down about them. Nature fascinates me with her colorful variety of life forms, landscapes, and celestial phenomena; I love to observe and capture spectacles of nature on a video camera. And what about music? Well, music is my safe haven; I just love to plunge into a fugue by Bach or an impromptu by Chopin and let the beautiful harmonies carry me away.

"I love to . . ." What does it really mean when we love someone or something? It's again a definition that we need here: **"To love" something is to cherish it unconditionally.** No strings attached. Whoever expects something in return for his/her love isn't loving at all, but is only scheming with his/her head. Yet **true love** always comes from the heart. It

Sixth Challenge: Love and Understanding

never takes, but always gives—without asking for anything. That's also the reason why true love can never end. A love that ends some day because it doesn't meet my expectations anymore would have been tied to a condition all along!

> I love you.
> Not because you're good looking.
> Not because you know a lot.
> Not because you're different.
> Not so that you love me too.
> I love you just as you are.
> Not for any reason.

This little poem describes my love for my wife just as it describes my love for our two sons. But it also describes my love for philosophy, for nature, and for music. I love nature as it is—I don't expect her to give me something in return. I also love gospel music as it is; it doesn't matter at all which country the choir is from or whether the singers are black or white or of any other color.

Love isn't just about what happens between two people. It's the unfathomable magic power that dwells within the cosmos and makes two things turn into one. So, here is how I'm going to define the noun *love*: **"Love" is the power that makes one out of two.** It already begins at the subatomic level! Three quarks together make a proton or a neutron, and we physicists call their underlying force "strong force." Next, protons and neutrons together make an atomic nucleus that—surrounded by a cloud of electrons—produces an entire atom. The positively charged protons exert a force on the negatively charged electrons that attracts. The attracting force is "electromagnetic force." Modern physics is aware of two more fundamental forces: "weak force" (which appears in nuclear fusion) and "gravitational force" (which makes masses attract each other). In figure 44, I sketched all four fundamental forces for you. Among them, strong force is the strongest followed by electromagnetic force, weak force, and gravitational force as the weakest.

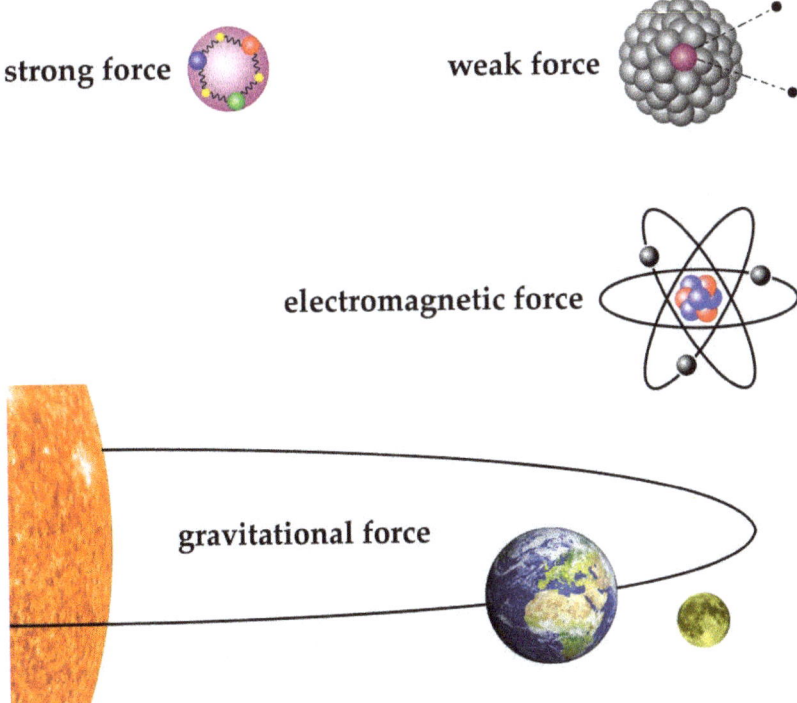

Fig. 44: The four fundamental forces of physics

Sixth Challenge: Love and Understanding

Most physicists assume that all four fundamental forces lead back to one common "primal force."[116] But no one has been successful so far in establishing a mathematical theory for this primal force. I also can't confirm my following claim yet scientifically, but I am convinced that someday it will prove to be the key interface between science and religion: *The primal force that we physicists are searching for so feverishly today is essentially identical with what we have already defined as love.* I stand by my claim, even when many of my colleagues will call on me to not combine physical concepts like "force" and "power" with religious concepts like "love." But these colleagues overlook an important fact: There is also a power in love, yet it can't be physically measured. Let me give you an example that clearly shows how strong the power of love is: Knowledge alone can't stop a war—only true love is able to do that!

The tremendous power of love permeates like an invisible bond through all the six material levels of nature (figure 45). On the first—and deepest—level, we suspect so-called *quarks*. They form on the second level the nuclear elements (namely protons and neutrons) which team up with a cloud of electrons on the third level to make atoms. On the fourth level, atoms then team up to make molecules, and on a fifth level, molecules team up to make cells. The sixth level is the outer manifestation of complex living things. As long as we dissect nature into various levels, it appears very reasonable to give a different name to each force depending on the level that it is acting on. But if we conceive nature as one big picture, we see that behind all of these forces one and the same engine moves everything: love.

True Love

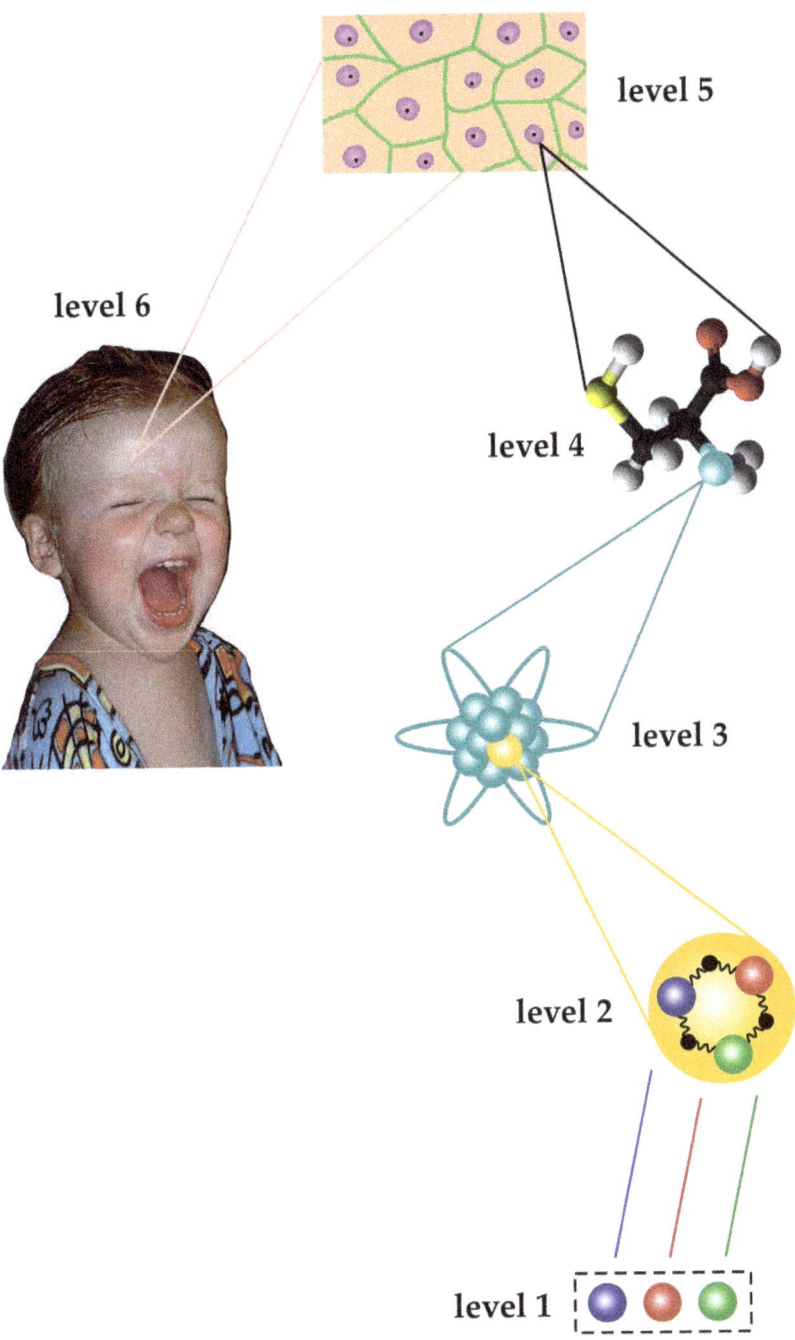

Fig. 45: The six material levels of nature

Sixth Challenge: Love and Understanding

By the way, an observation already made by Greek philosopher Aristotle backs up my claim: The whole is always greater than the sum of its parts.[117] The following examples show that Aristotle is right: A DNA molecule can store genetic information, an atom cannot. A cell can communicate, a molecule cannot. A human being can think, a cell cannot. Yet what causes atoms, molecules, and cells to team up to make a whole? What drives the atoms to team up to make molecules? What drives the molecules to team up to make cells? And what drives the cells to team up to make complex living things like us?

Everywhere in nature we find a willingness that strives to team up for something greater. So much teamwork can only be achieved by a fundamental concept—I call it "love." And the more I think about it, the more this primal force that moves everything takes shape: By acting on every level of nature and making two things into one that is more than the sum of its parts, this force is continually creating added value. In this way, love is pursuing the highest goal that is worth striving for in the cosmos. With an unbiased mind, we might want to call it "divine."

True Understanding

Love is a central part of many religions. It is the true heart of Christianity. But physics isn't able to deal with love. I clearly remember a conversation that I had more than ten years ago with a member of the Faculty of Physics and Astronomy at my university. The faculty actually wanted me to revoke my teaching permit because I was combining physics with religion in my books. The colleague explained to me that we have been able to understand all of this world with physics alone and didn't need the additional help of God or eternity. So, I asked him only one question: "How can love be understood with physics?" His reaction was so disgraceful and below the office of a university that I felt that I was blown back to the dark ages: "Mr. Niemz—there is the door!" How wise of that faculty to no longer pursue its purpose. The lifeblood of every university is to promote knowledge among all of its disciplines.

In the meantime, the sheer magnitude of my question that came to me out of the blue dawned on me. Can love be understood at all? We often talk of "love and understanding" in one breath. But why? Because "love" is emotional and "understanding" is rational—and we then believe that we've covered all of the aspects of life? Let me put the corresponding definitions side by side:

"To love" something is to cherish it unconditionally.	"To understand" something is to share its perspective.
"Love" is the power that makes one out of two.	"Understanding" is participating in something.

So, there might be a simple answer to the question why we can't understand love: It's the language of God, and we just can't share God's perspective.

Sixth Challenge: Love and Understanding

Now, let's look for examples for something that we can actually understand. A good friend of yours can understand how you feel and react in a specific situation if he/she shares your perspective. He/she then participates in your life, that is, he/she sympathizes with you.

We can also try to put ourselves into the perspectives of people we don't know who may not be as fortunate as we are. How would a displaced person feel who is fleeing out of fear from oppression or hunger into our country? We can also sympathize with his/her fate, right? Wouldn't we do the same thing if we were in his/her situation?

But understanding isn't just about living things. We can also try to understand processes in nature. We already know a perfect example, and I'm now taking it up again in order to demonstrate **true understanding**: natural selection during biological evolution. Only those species survive that have learned to live in harmony with nature. Charles Darwin had *truly understood* this fundamental principle of natural selection and described it in full detail. Every species that does not adjust to its environment will sooner or later be excluded from evolution. All observations today support Darwin's theory so much that we may indeed consider it true understanding. Biological species are formed through very small mutations that can prove to be beneficial or not beneficial. We remember: A few decades before Darwin's revelation, Jean-Baptiste Lamarck still believed that a "nervous fluid" would extend a giraffe's neck.

Unfortunately, the evolution of life has often been *misunderstood* on one key point. We're talking again about the role of chance. In our fourth challenge on chicken and egg, I contrasted Darwin's theory with the theory of an intelligent design when I identified coincidence (mutations by chance) as the motor for Darwin's theory and order (a given design) as the motor for an intelligent design. So far, so good! But Darwin's skeptics—with the creationists leading the way—justly invoke even to this day the right to claim that the present complexity of life couldn't have come about by chance alone. For example, the human genome is made up of about three billion *base pairs*.[118] One base pair in the double strand of DNA consists of two opposing *nucleobases* (A, C, G, T). In the DNA, there are four possible combinations per base pair: AT, TA, CG, and GC. So, there are $4^{3,000,000,000}$ different possibilities about how a genome with three billion base pairs can appear. And that means: If Mother Nature makes one new genome every second, one would expect that she is busy for $4^{3,000,000,000}$ seconds (this is equal to about $10^{1,800,000,000}$ years!) creating my genome. For comparison: The Bing Bang was only 10^{10} years ago.

We know that Darwin already had a very important insight: There was no need for nature to create my genome all at once. She could have made it happen gradually—during variations in minute progressions. The difference that we're sketching here is tremendous, and we must really thank the British evolutionary biologist Richard Dawkins for giving us this (supposedly true) understanding. Dawkins refers to it as *cumulative selection*.[119] Whenever a specific gene mutation proves itself, thus bringing an advantage with it for the species involved, then nature doesn't always have to "invent" it again and again. The successful mutation is simply transmitted to the following generation. So, for our example: Since there are only four possibilities per base pair, nature already has "found" after four seconds the first base pair of my genome (which is then inherited); after another four seconds, the second; after another four seconds, the third, and so on. In this case, nature has created my complete genome in only 4 x 3,000,000,000 seconds—and that's only about 380 years! This is why it actually took longer: In nature, not one mutation occurs every second, but a few mutations occur every generation.

So, nature has to "invent" every base pair only once *by chance;* after that, it is inherited in *ordered* manner (according to specific rules). But Dawkins oversteps his bounds whenever he downplays the role that chance plays in his concept of cumulative selection. He writes: "This belief, that Darwinian evolution is 'random', is not merely false. It is the exact opposite of the truth. Chance is a minor ingredient in the Darwinian recipe, but the most important ingredient is cumulative selection which is quintessentially *non*-random."[120] Dawkins is actually saying that heredity is an orderly process and consequently relegates chance from evolution. That isn't correct, however, because the determining process for the evolution of any new species isn't heredity, but genetic mutation, and it always happens spontaneously—by chance. So, chance plays a key role in evolution, but order is added to it. This fits perfectly well to what we found in our fourth challenge: Life is based on a very creative mix of both order and chance.

The fact that evolution can't succeed without chance can be identified in still another element that we had already discussed in our fifth challenge: the very first element z_1 in a

True Understanding

recursive algorithm. The concept of evolution is composed mathematically of two assumptions: 1) There will be at some time or other a world's first living species (an element z_1). 2) From any species A (an element z_n) a new species B (an element z_{n+1}) can evolve. Both Darwin and Dawkins are reflecting almost exclusively on the second assumption, and they are doing it on a very high scientific level. But neither Darwin nor Dawkins comes up with specific ideas whenever we begin to scrutinize the first assumption: Where did the very first element z_1 come from?

I've already given the answer, and I'm gladly repeating it here again because it demonstrates beautifully what real understanding is all about—participation. We participate in how the evolution of life actually works. Now, here is my answer again: Matter is either not alive or alive. So, the transition from one to the other *must* have been spontaneous (by chance), which tells us that it had no cause at all. The very first element z_1 came into this world by chance. But it would be premature to conclude that there isn't anything divine. I'd like to remind you of our third challenge: Whatever happens by chance is a creative act in itself since it isn't caused by anything else. Spontaneity is the epitome of creativity. For this very reason, a cosmos in which life just happens is as creative as any God can be.

So now we have some idea how evolution started. But where is evolution going—is there an ultimate element z_{final}? Well, that element probably doesn't exist because, according to the second assumption, the algorithm can always make another element $z_{final+1}$. And to point out how everything fits together, our reflections on space and time bring us to the same conclusion: There is no end to time; so, the evolution of life can continue to advance at random. But evolution on earth can and certainly will end at some time or other, and at the latest in about five billion years when our sun will have expanded itself all the way to a *red giant* until it completely engulfs our planet.[121]

Chance ensures that no one—not even God—can plan where the cosmic journey of life leads. Instead of our human genomes, evolution on earth could have generated entirely different genomes in the past 4.6 billion years. So, it is very unlikely that we would ever encounter the same species on other planets like the ones we find here on earth. Dawkins himself talks about a *blind watchmaker* who makes things in the universe, but can't see.[122] The watchmaker-analogy goes back as early as William Paley, Darwin's great role model. Richard Dawkins puts the cherry on the cake in a very intuitive way when he adds the attribute "blind" that connects design ("watchmaker") with chance ("blind").

So far, we haven't yet focused on an important aspect of evolution: death. Whoever wants to understand how evolution works shouldn't ignore this uncomfortable theme. It's even helpful to come to grips with the topic of death during one's life because it loses the fear that we might feel as soon as we understand why it's necessary. In theory (for example, in a computer simulation), the recursive algorithm of evolution also works with cells that live forever, but it fails in real life: A limited habitat with life, like planet earth, wouldn't have enough room for all emerging generations. In order to live, we would have to compete with each other for available space and all the resources necessary for life.

But death comes with an active purpose too: It ensures natural selection so that the evolution of life can advance. Species with genetic mutations that prove to be unfavorable for life will eventually die out. This is how nature succeeds at being so effective—to economize valuable resources in a sustained manner while advancing *biologically* at the same time. But what stays hidden from most people is that death contributes essentially to *spiritual* evolution too: Why should we do something today if we could still do it tomorrow? It's death that makes us not put off until tomorrow what we can do today. So, try to *understand* death once in a while from this perspective—and it will become more likeable for you! Death is not an enemy of life. It's rather the mortality of life that moves us and makes consciousness grow in the cosmos.

True Happiness

It happened on the way to work this morning. I was moving along with other commuters through the narrow subway at Mannheim Central Station when it flashed right in front of my feet. I bent down and picked up a shiny one-euro coin. "My lucky day!", I thought to myself. But then "bang!"—a heavy suitcase hit me from behind and hurt my right heel. I squirmed and limped painfully to the exit. A few moments later, while walking in pain, I was struck how the artificial neon light gave way to warm daylight beyond it. There sat a man on his blanket playing a clarinet. Most people went by and didn't even take notice of him. I stopped, and instantly harmonic sounds captured my imagination.

Sixth Challenge: Love and Understanding

Like magic, the music made me forget my pain. When the clarinet stopped playing, I felt the warm coin nestled in my hand and put it in the cardboard box in front of the musician. He thanked me with a smile that made all of his face beam with joy. In that very moment, I understood the tremendous difference between *lucky* and *happy*. Most people associate both concepts with joy, and some languages like German have only one word to fit both. But I can tell you: There are no two concepts more different than these! When I found the one-euro coin, I was lucky—not happy. I found it only because someone else had the bad luck to lose it. I was only happy after I gave the same coin to someone who really needed it.

Here's a little quiz question for you: What's still vivid in my mind whenever I remember that morning in Mannheim? Just one answer is correct:

a) the pain in my right heel,
b) the artificial neon light,
c) the musician's smile.

You got it right—it's the beaming smile of the musician! Memories of the pain in my heel and also the neon light have long since faded. It's too bad that most people associate *both* lucky and happy with joy. If we took a closer look at both concepts, we wouldn't fall so quickly into the temptation of confusing material *having* luck with immaterial *being* happy. This confusion is the main reason why people fail in their search for becoming happy and live lives of silent desperation instead (figure 46).

True Happiness

Fig. 46: Lucky or happy?

Let's take a closer look at some more examples to clarify the difference between lucky and happy: If you have a job, have a house, have lots of contacts—then you are lucky. If you are pleased with what you do, are at home everywhere you go, are always among friends—then you are happy. All these situations describe lucky as something that you *have*, but happy describes what you *are*. Happy is not what you have, it's what you are! Be honest—have you ever thought this much about being truly happy?

Unfortunately, we live in an age today that puts more value on luck—not happiness. TV shows like *Who Wants to Be a Millionaire?* and excessive lotto jackpots make more and more people dream of striking it rich—hitting "the big one." But this luck is just luck that I can *have* or *not have*—it's not the **true happiness** deep in my heart that lets me *be* happy. Having luck never goes deep because I can just as easily lose again whatever I have. Only what I am right here and now, no one can take away from me. It's what I am—now!

Sixth Challenge: Love and Understanding

The search for true happiness is something that really brings us all together. In order to see this, here is a simple trick. Please ask yourself: Can I imagine anything in life that is more worth striving for than being happy? And if such a thing really exists, wouldn't I strive for it precisely for this reason because I expect that it will make me happy? After you have answered these two questions, you will know that we all strive—deep in our hearts—for the same goal: being happy! Please meditate about this insight for a few minutes because it transforms us all into social beings: We all want to be happy, and that brings us all together. The fact that we often get in each other's way is because most people don't know how this true happiness can be found. They hope to come upon it somewhere in their lives and don't see that it is already inside of them.

How do I become happy? Believe it or not—there is a clear answer to this question, and that is why I made it my motto of life. Since happy is something that I am and don't have, there is nothing outside of me (no other living thing, no object, no event) that can make me happy. There is only one recipe to be happy:

I am happy
if I say "yes" to everything that I *am* (not: *have*)
and—with this attitude—take my next step forward.

It's just as easy as it sounds. I only have to accept me as I am and then live with this attitude, and I am already happy. But if I say "no"—for example, because I want to *have* a more beautiful body or fancier clothes or a better job—then I am unhappy. Just try it yourself. It really works! But now you could argue: If everyone says "yes" to oneself, the motivation will be lost to change something. That is why it is so important to not only say "yes" to oneself, but—from being happy—to also take the next step forward. Most people believe that being happy is the true goal of life, but it isn't—it's the path! I often like to put it this way: Enlightenment isn't about searching for becoming happy, but about living one's happiness step by step.

And so, being happy or not being happy has absolutely nothing to do with my environment. It has everything to do with myself and, most of all, it is a matter of heart: If I welcome all of the experiences of life, then I am happy. Never forget: It's the mind that says "no" to some things and consequently makes us unhappy. By the way, it's precisely for this reason that people meditate—to let go of their thoughts. Meditation is actually nothing more than a universal yes-saying to everything that is.

Let's remember Alfred North Whitehead and his *drops of experience*. We are these drops of experience, and we are happy if we welcome all drops of experience, that is, if we welcome each other. Yet this yes-saying to everything that is also means surrender. In an age characterized by rabid consumption and greed, it would do us much good to practice surrender. This could involve our own interests in partnerships[123] or salary increases. The well-known saying "being perfectly happy" isn't by chance. It is based upon the great treasure troves cherished from many generations of experience and implies that true happiness occurs whenever we are free of wishes and desires.

Sixth Challenge: Love and Understanding

Love and Understanding Are Not Two

The moment is finally here—the big moment when we can taste the fruits of our work. One key message of this book is that we aren't any nouns, but verbs: "human becomings." According to Alfred North Whitehead, we may equate ourselves with experiencing, that is, with feeling and learning. If we now combine this knowledge with our discovery from the end of challenge 4 ("everything is interacting with its environment"), we are in the midst of lifting a very precious treasure—the answer to the riddle about ourselves: **"I" am a feeling-with-others and a learning-with-others.**

So we exist in a giant network—the network of Mother Nature! In my connection with others, far more can actually be accomplished than by myself. It's too bad that this guiding principle of nature is undermined today by many people and populist parties, as they put themselves, their "individuality," and their own nations first. But what they don't see: No one can be truly happy with a world view that fails to understand our true nature. We need to unite rather than to compete in order to solve all these global conflicts that exist today on earth.

In nature, two other values stand at the top that we can derive immediately from our treasure: love and understanding. Love is based upon *compassion* ("feeling with others"). Understanding is based upon *joint knowledge* ("learning with others"). Yes, that's true! Even for our understanding, we depend on others—on teachers, for example. And since both values stand at the very top of nature's scale, they must not benefit anyone, that is, they make sense *in themselves*. I don't exaggerate if I claim that a fixed expression of our language corresponds directly to the meaning of life:

> Love and understanding
> are the true meaning of life.

Whoever internalizes this meaning can regard himself or herself to be truly happy. And by the way, this testimony agrees beautifully with reports of the dying. They often talk about a bright light that emanates "unconditional love" and "infinite knowledge."[124] If you would like to learn more, I'm happy to entrust a special reading for you in the following bonus chapter.

The correct scientific term for "compassion" is *empathy*. But "compassion" actually comes from the Greek word *sympatheia* (in English: sympathy). Equally enlightening for us is the Latin word for "joint knowledge": *conscientia* (in English: consciousness). Sympathy and consciousness lead us to the true meaning of life![125]

It can be easily shown that the true meaning of life can't consist of having a lot of money, wearing expensive clothes, driving fast cars, or staying in 5-star hotels. It also has nothing to do with being a good Christian, Muslim, Jew, Hindu, or Buddhist. Why not? The true meaning of life must have been valid for creatures, too, that lived on earth millions of years ago. Those creatures could already feel and learn; so, they could give birth to love and understanding. But back at that time, there was no money yet, also no clothes, no cars, no hotels, no Christians, no Muslims, no Jews, no Hindus, and no Buddhists.

Sixth Challenge: Love and Understanding

To wrap things up, I finally quote a great teacher who completely internalized what we have just uncovered about the true meaning of life. Tenzin Gyatso, the 14th Dalai Lama, teaches us: "Ethics is more important than religion."[126] How true! But to hear this sentence from a spiritual leader who belittles the significance of his own "religion" for the sake of truth must be so altruistic and honorable that we really have to hand it to him. No other spiritual leader—neither in religion nor in politics—has ever so self-critically put his own authority in such a clear perspective. Gyatso is not advertising his own philosophy of life, Buddhism. Of his own free will, he changes the perspective and has come far closer to the *truth* with this trick than any pope or president.

Many conflicts flare up in our world because of *religious self-delusion,* and I have already described this delusion in a previous book.[127] Mandatory ethics classes could help to fix these problems, similar to the way we teach native language as a basic subject in school. Only those who can objectively compare all religions together will value freedom of religion and give support to it for his or her fellow men and women. These ethics classes should motivate us to evaluate a student's involvement for the good of others—not the output that someone gets for himself or herself.

Tenzin Gyatso calls ethics the "science of happiness."[128] He advises us to use compassion as much as possible as we train our own *mirror neurons.* Mirror neurons are specialized nerve cells in the brain that are responsible for empathetic behavior. There is evidence that such training is really possible. We only need to look at the results of a study[129] from 2004. In this study, scientists investigated the brain activity of monks. The results are stunning: During a deep meditation—a phase of high mindfulness—high-frequency gamma waves dominate the *electroencephalogram (EEG)*. While being awake, people who aren't mindful have mid-frequency beta waves; while being asleep, people have low-frequency theta waves (figure 47). My research group at Heidelberg University is currently investigating how we can train our gamma waves in a specified manner. Please email me if you would like to support our research or if you wish to invite me to a reading. You can find my address at the end of the book.

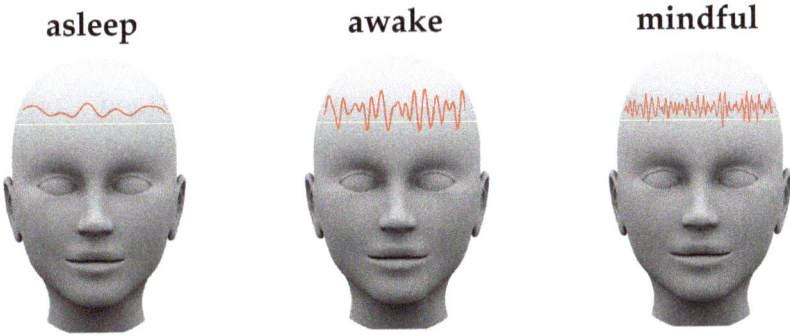

Fig. 47: EEG activity in the human brain

Tenzin Gyatso's message is so significant for humanity that I must repeat it again here. I will even extend it to two other segments of human life that are equally important—economics and politics.

> Ethics is more important than religion.
> Nature is more important than industry.
> Human rights are more important than patriotism.

Sixth Challenge: Love and Understanding

In order to catch up with Gyatso, the head of a company would have to voluntarily admit that the environment is more important than his own company; and the president of a country would have to announce that human rights for all would be more important than the interests of his own people. Will humanity live to see businessmen and politicians who are like this? It's humanity's hope because, in the age of globalization, we can survive only if we understand that our future will depend on other living things—and the future of many other living things will depend on us. We're making a big mistake if we believe that industry would always have to thrive or a country would have to take action against refugees or dissidents. To survive as a species we must learn to live in harmony with Mother Nature. To understand Mother Nature we must learn to share the perspective of others—by feeling and learning with them!

Love springs from understanding—and understanding springs from love. We have encountered the same interplay with chicken/egg and Yin/Yang (see figures 23 and 41). Love and understanding are our final non-duality.

Message of our sixth challenge:
*There is no love without understanding,
and no understanding without love.*

Alternative ways to express this message:
*Love and understanding are not two.
Love and understanding are two sides of the same coin.*

The coin's name is: *truth*.

I say thank you for joining me on this philosophical journey. We reached our final destination—the true meaning of life. As a reward, I am handing you all the gleaming coins that we have collected together in our six challenges (figure 48). Take very good care of them!

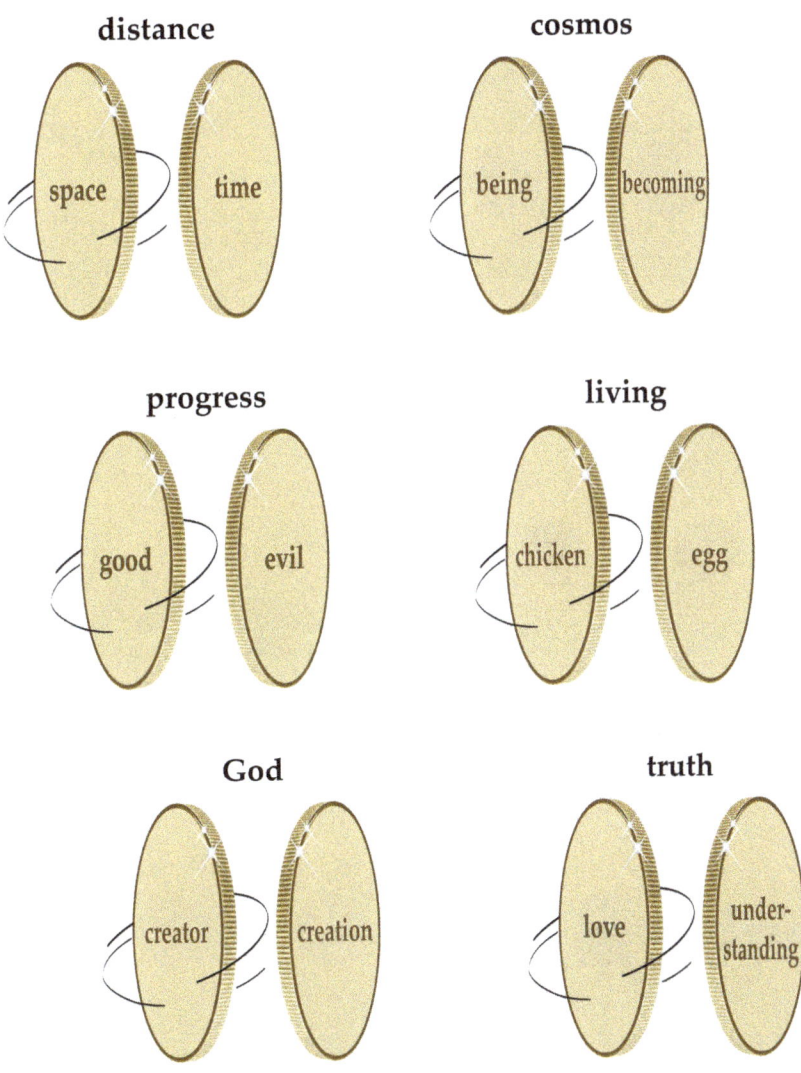

Fig. 48: The coins from our six challenges

Bonus Chapter

Einstein's Relativity and Near-Death Experiences

It is October 1987. At Heidelberg University, I am attending a seminar on Einstein's theory of relativity and we are currently discussing the relativity of spatial and temporal distances. Figure 49 shows how Albert Einstein is traveling in a spaceship from the earth to the moon approximately 300,000 kilometers away. Someone else—I call him Mr. Zweistein—is watching the flight from earth. We assume that the spaceship is moving at a very high[130] velocity—at 99.995 percent of the speed of light. With these numerical values, the entire flight takes about a second on Mr. Zweistein's watch.

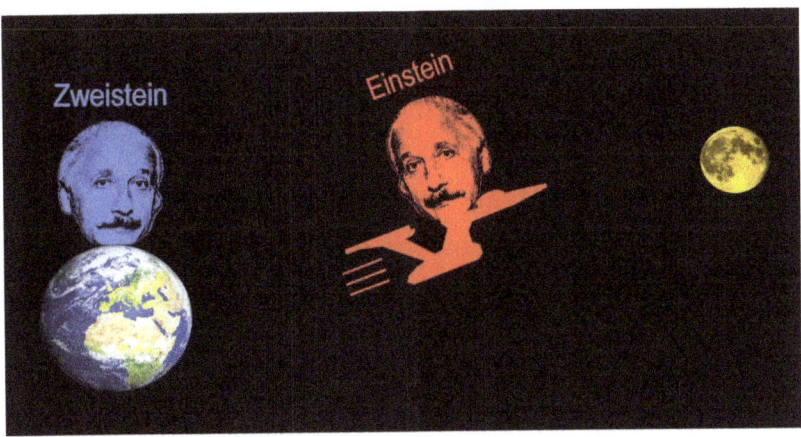

Fig. 49: Albert Einstein is traveling to the moon

But from Mr. Einstein's perspective and with the same flight speed, the distance between the earth and the moon reduces to about 3,000 kilometers because his spaceship is moving relative to this distance. So, on Einstein's watch, the entire flight takes only .01 seconds. If a fictitious spaceship could fly at 100 percent of the speed of light, the theory of relativity even predicts that the distance between the earth and the moon would be zero, which means the entire flight would last zero seconds.

Just as we were coming up with the results of this event in our seminar, a young student asked this question: "If no time elapses for a spaceship traveling at the speed of light, isn't light in eternity?" Unfortunately, this question seemed to overwhelm our physics professor. He replied that eternity is not a physical concept and advised that student to attend a theological seminar. Yet still to this day, I doubt whether in such a seminar I would have got a conclusive answer to *my* question.

Today, more than thirty years after this seminar, I am firmly convinced that *being-within-the-light* actually equates with eternity. But it's not quite correct to say "time does not go by" in the light. If all temporal distance has the value of zero in light, then all of our time elapses in light in a single instant. So, eternity isn't timelessness, but *timerichness*. Everything that has ever happened in the cosmos is present in the light!

Many people associate the concept "eternity" with life and death, but aren't aware that there are striking parallels between Einstein's relativity and so-called *near-death experiences*. This is now our theme. **A "near-death experience" is a phenomenon that can occur (but not always) if someone comes very near death and, after successful resuscitation, recalls what was experienced.**[131] Accidents and heart attacks are very typical situations for such a near-death experience to occur. Because more and more people today survive an acute cardiac arrest thanks to modern emergency medicine, the recent number of near-death reports has increased significantly. Fifty years ago, most of the people affected died before they could share their experiences.[132] But never forget: Only a person who has had a near-death experience can judge what he or she experienced. Mainstream medicine is making a big mistake whenever it doesn't take the people affected seriously and writes off their experiences as hallucinations. Kenneth Ring, an American investigator of near-death, suggests that we should divide these experiences into five stages:[133]

– feeling painlessness and peace (stage 1),
– an out-of-body experience (stage 2),
– moving through a dark tunnel (stage 3),
– encountering a bright light (stage 4),
– plunging into the light, experiencing a life review (stage 5).

So now I will explain how stages 3 and 4 can be interpreted through a physical effect. After that, I will comment on the life review. Let's assume it is a still day in the middle of the winter and it's snowing. You are sitting in the front seat of a car and traveling at a high speed with snowflakes falling. Someone else who observes the scene from the side of the road sees a car that is moving from left to right (figure 50 top). And he or she also sees snowflakes falling vertically from above to below because the wind is still. Compared to the car moving at a high speed, the snowflakes fall slowly— indicated by shorter arrows.

What does the same scene look like from your perspective in the car? Well, the car isn't moving at all relative to your body. Instead, everything outside of the car is moving past you—the landscape and all the falling snowflakes. Because the relative speed between the car and the snowflakes is independent from perspective, you project the speed of the car onto the speed of the snowflakes. That's why, from your perspective, the snowflakes are falling at a high speed *and* slanted onto the windshield (the arrows in the bottom of figure 50 are longer).

Fig. 50: Analogy to the searchlight effect

What you just read is a perfect analogy to an effect of Einstein's theory of relativity that isn't as well known as the relativity of space and time: the *searchlight effect*.[134] But it is just as fascinating! Let's simply replace the snowflakes with light and the car with a rocket: From the perspective of an observer outside of the rocket, light hits the rocket from all directions including from the sides (figure 51 top). From the rocket's perspective, all surrounding light rushes in from the front—bundled like a searchlight (figure 51 bottom). Arrow length doesn't change here since the speed of light is always constant. So, a passenger in the rocket sees almost all darkness from all sides. Most of the light is approaching from the front—he or she is indeed looking into a dark tunnel with a bright light at the end of it.

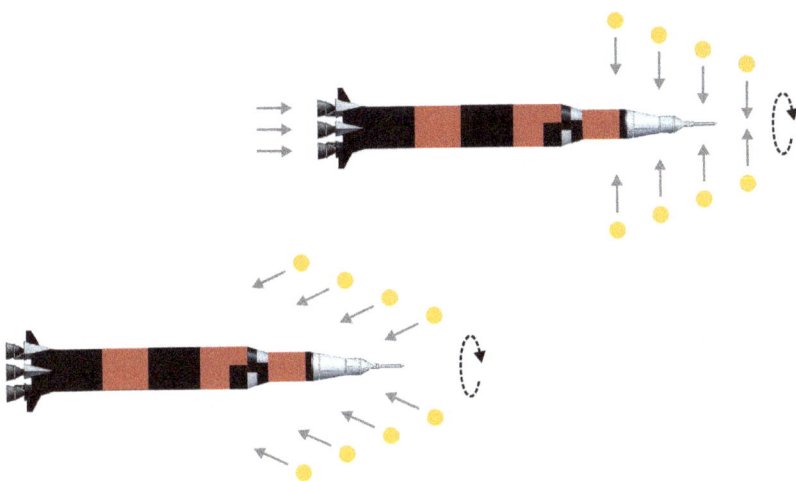

Fig. 51: The searchlight effect

Figures 52 and 53 illustrate how the searchlight effect becomes noticeable when traveling at almost the speed of light. What you see here is a flight through a historic district of half-timbered houses in Tuebingen, Germany.[135] The pictures show a physically exact simulation based on Einstein's theory of relativity.

Bonus Chapter

Fig. 52a: Flight without searchlight effect (75 percent of c)

Fig. 52b: Flight without searchlight effect (95 percent of c)

Fig. 52c: Flight without searchlight effect (99 percent of c)

Fig. 53a: Flight with searchlight effect (75 percent of c)

Fig. 53b: Flight with searchlight effect (95 percent of c)

Fig. 53c: Flight with searchlight effect (99 percent of c)

Bonus Chapter

The simulation shown in figures 52 and 53 is physically exact in the sense that it takes into account the finite speed of light (a finite travel time) and the searchlight effect. For a better understanding of the figures, I would like to give you three more details: 1) In physics, the symbol c denotes the speed of light. 2) The scenes were zoomed-in as the speed was increasing to also account for the forward motion while the rocket is in flight. 3) The bending of the houses is a result of the finite light travel time—light that was reflected from the ground floors reaches the rocket in an earlier time than light from the roofs.[136]

The searchlight effect clearly gives us the impression of a tunnel with a light at the other end. For the first time, near-death experiences that describe a tunnel and a light can be interpreted as *real experiences*—we only need to assume that some part of us plunges into the light while we die.[137] For example, Craig reports after he had nearly drowned on a rafting trip: "It was like a *tunnel*. I seemed to be picking up speed. I felt as if I were moving *at the speed of light* through the blackness. Far away in the distance, I could see a small *pinpoint of light* that seemed to be growing larger ... It was not long before it engulfed me, and I felt as if I became one with the light. It seemed to have knowledge of everything there is to know, and it accepted me as part of it. I felt all-knowing for a few minutes. The whole world seemed to be in total harmony."[138] What's remarkable is—with plunging into the light, the mysterious *life review* that is often reported can be understood.[139] The dying person "bathes" in the light, feeling again all of the scenes experienced during an entire lifetime. This becomes possible because of the memory effect of light that we discussed in challenge 2. Upon dying, the life review confronts us with our own life that is stored in the light. We get mirrored with all the love that we gave to others and all the pain that we caused to others. No external God will judge us on doomsday, but we will be our own judge, after we view our own lives in the light of the big picture. Justice can't be any fairer nor more divine than this! Now here comes my advice: *Live your life in such a way that your review will be as pleasant as possible.*

You could argue that the searchlight effect accidentally resembles the tunnel experience of those who are dying. But then is it a second coincidence that this tunnel makes a beeline into the light and eternity? Is it a third coincidence that in the light everyone is confronted with their own life because the light "knows" everything? And is it even a fourth coincidence that eternity is forbidden to all material things because matter is always physically slower than light?

I must be honest—it is difficult for me to believe that all this is only coincidence. It's more likely that there is indeed a connection among all of these phenomena: 1) The searchlight effect explains the tunnel experience that many dying people are reporting. 2) Some part of us plunges into the light while we die; the tunnel is a kind of bridge to eternity. 3) Everything is stored in the light—all laws of nature and all of my life. 4) It isn't worth striving for material things. These four clues fit together like the pieces of a jigsaw puzzle: *There's "something" around us and everywhere in outer space that guarantees the laws of nature and keeps track of every single move that we make. This "something" stands above all things.* It is . . . light!

Talk with the Author

Professor Niemz, you are a full professor of biomedical engineering at the oldest university in Germany. You are not only a successful researcher, but also a gifted author and speaker. Why do you write spiritual books?

Niemz: Life fascinates me. Just like everyone else, I would also like to know where we come from, why we're here and where we go someday. My profession requires a lot of investigating into the subject of light, and light itself also holds an extremely powerful fascination upon me. I think of light as cosmic memory. It stores everything that has ever happened in the cosmos. But it gets even more thrilling whenever we ask about the nature of light. What is light? Neither scientists nor theologians can answer this seemingly simple question. Is this the reason why world religions equate light with the divine—with God? There's one thing that we know for sure about light, and we owe a great debt of gratitude to Albert Einstein for it: Within all light, each spatial distance and each temporal distance turns zero. Just think about it! Try to fathom the valuable message hidden in this one sentence! It means that everything in the cosmos is intimate to the light since it is all "here" for the light. It also means that everything in the cosmos is familiar to the light since it is all "now" for the light. If we put these two statements together, we get: A God, who has access to light's memory, loves us all and knows it all! And now we have already built a bridge from modern physics to religion—not made from steel and concrete, but from spiritual thoughts.

You know how to present complex connectedness of things intuitively. Upon listening to you, we get a feeling for those things that really matter. Should we think more in terms of connectivity?

Niemz: Well, when I look at today's world, I honestly think that we pay far too little attention to connectedness. It's often right in front of us and so obvious. We only have to get a feeling of how one thing effects another. Thank heavens that most of us have learned by now that our lifestyle influences the world climate. But now, the fastest actions possible must follow as a consequence of what we've learned. Even in our daily lives we would be very wise to heed connectedness of things: Whoever is always trying to get his way will never have a successful partnership. Whoever exercises power will never live in peace. Whoever excludes other human beings will never understand the big picture. The cosmos and every living thing that it embraces are an inseparable, continually unfolding process.

Does connectivity also reveal something about life after death?

Niemz: Absolutely! At this point, I always like to quote the American biologist Bruce Lipton: "If you were just a spirit, what does chocolate taste like?" Lipton wants to illustrate how empty a life would be in which I can no longer perceive anything without my body. I fully agree with Lipton since I myself wouldn't consider that as "life" anymore. Even so, I show in my book that there truly is an eternity. It does not let me live on after death, but it embraces even the smallest thought and feeling of the life that I'm living now.

Talk with the Author

Where do you obtain your knowledge about eternity? Have you ever had some crucial experience?

Niemz: Yes, I've even had two of those crucial experiences. During the first one, I somehow "perceived" how my wife's father died 100 kilometers away. I can't explain it scientifically even to this day. A few days after my two parents had died, I had my second experience: Of course, I would have loved to tell my parents so many more things until it suddenly became clear to me how pointless such a communication would be. What news could I share with them if everything is known in eternity? They would have already known it anyway!!! Take your time and just think about it. This one thought fundamentally transformed my conception of eternity. It doesn't make me sad—but happy—and it gives me strength. Now I know that all of those perfect moments that I was able to share with my dear parents are enshrined forever in eternity. It's not me who's immortal, but the life that I live ... is!

I thought that Christians believe in resurrection. Don't you have to believe in eternal life as a Christian?

Niemz: I'd rather leave the belief in personal survival after death to all those who deem themselves as indispensable. I don't know of any bible verse that truly holds out the prospect of life after death for us. I suggest that we rethink our conception of the adjective "eternal": It doesn't mean "existing in time unbounded," but "always recallable within the light."

Talk with the Author

Professor Niemz, your new book describes the beginning of life as a random act—something that wasn't caused by anything. Is life on earth something unique in the universe?

Niemz: Not necessarily, because we physicists assume that radioactivity is a random event, too, and radioactive decays occur countless times throughout the universe. And so, the beginning of life could also repeat itself again and again—provided that conditions are suitable on any given planet. But I still thank you for this question. I actually conceive life as a random, cosmic act. And for a very good reason: Matter is either not alive or alive. So, the transition from one to the other must have been spontaneous, which tells us that it had no cause at all. Everything that isn't caused, but happens on its own, we commonly designate as "chance."

Please give our readers a few short statements to wrap things up—your favorite pastime?

Niemz: To live.

Your favorite place?

Niemz: Here.

Your most beautiful occasion?

Niemz: Now.

Your favorite dish?

Niemz: Swiss hash browns with vegetables and cheese.

Do you have any role models?

Niemz: Next to Charles Darwin and Albert Einstein you'll find again and again another name in my book that is not as well known—Alfred North Whitehead. This British mathematician and philosopher taught me that there's no "individual myself" and no "individual yourself." There's only a "cosmic ourselves"—the sum of all experiencing in the cosmos. It's precisely this ourselves that we should cherish and embrace instead of clinging to an illusionary individuality.

What does happiness really mean to you?

Niemz: Happiness is what we're all searching for. For some, it's love. For others, it's understanding, beauty, fulfillment, peace, wealth. However, many people don't become happy in their search for happiness because they confuse "having" with "being." Since happy is something that I am and don't have, there is nothing outside of me that can make me happy. So, it is completely up to me whether I am happy or not. I am happy if I say "yes" to everything that I am and—with this attitude—take my next step forward. Being happy isn't the goal of life—it's the path!

Thank you, Professor Niemz, for this inspiring conversation.

Author's website: http://www.markolfniemz.de/en
Contact address: markolf.niemz@lucys-kinder.de

Definitions Used in This Book

Page 20: "Time" is what I read off my watch.

Page 20: "Space" is what I read off my ruler.

Page 21: Something is "absolute" if it does not depend on the observer's perspective.

Page 28: Something is "relative" if it depends on the observer's perspective.

Page 42: "Reality" is how I perceive the world in space and time.

Page 48: From my perspective, "history" is anything that happened before "my now."

Page 48: From my perspective, "live" is anything that's happening at "my now."

Page 56: "Temporal distance" between two events is the amount of time that is needed to exchange information among them.

Page 56: "Spatial distance" is the same amount of time as in temporal distance, but multiplied by the speed of light.

Page 57: "Being" stands for anything that is neither spatial nor temporal.

Page 57: "Becoming" stands for anything that is spatial and/or temporal.

Definitions Used in This Book

Page 58: "Eternity" is being within the light.

Page 62: Something is "eternal" if it can always be recalled within the light.

Page 67: Something happens "by order" if something else causes it to happen.

Page 67: Something happens "by chance" if it happens by itself.

Page 82: "Good" is anything that improves things from my perspective.

Page 82: "Evil" is anything that makes things worse from my perspective.

Page 143: "To love" something is to cherish it unconditionally.

Page 144: "Love" is the power that makes one out of two.

Page 149: "To understand" something is to share its perspective.

Page 149: "Understanding" is participating in something.

Page 160: "I" am a feeling-with-others and a learning-with-others.

Page 168: A "near-death experience" is a phenomenon that can occur (but not always) if someone comes very near death and, after successful resuscitation, recalls what was experienced.

"Cultivate a sense of empathy.
Put yourself in other people's shoes.
See the world from their eyes."[140]
Barack Obama

Lucy's Children Foundation

Non-profit foundations can beat self-delusion—without the red tape. They promote projects that benefit society. Who can pass on love and understanding to others? Only those who have experienced love and understanding themselves! The willingness to commit yourself for the benefit of others must start at a young age—in the schools! *Lucy's Children Foundation* wants to open doors to love and understanding for poor children too: love through affection, understanding through education. If these children think in the same way when they're older, even the smallest contribution will multiply and bear fruit for the future.

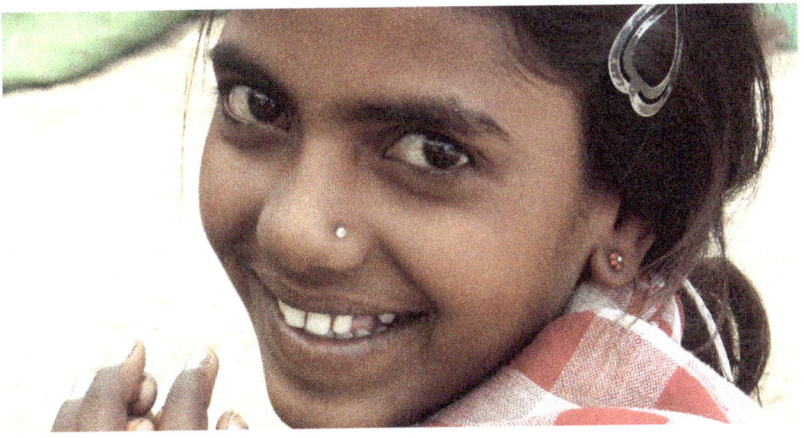

Fig. 54: Love through affection

Lucy's Children Foundation

Fig. 55: Understanding through education

Thinking holistically is good—living holistically is even better! I consider this to be the greatest challenge for humanity: to establish schools worldwide—schools that guarantee a thorough general education for all of us. "General" means that instruction would not be permitted to be influenced by any ideology, but it would compare political and religious convictions objectively. In order to fulfill this high aspiration in good faith, public and clerical school officials must renounce all political and missionary doctrines or goals. Only in this way can the young generation recognize for itself how valuable democracy and freedom of religion really are. And only in this way will things succeed to abolish hatred in the world and to strengthen our sense of community. Education should always be about experiencing things for oneself. This is why I do *not* offer any new religion in my books, but I encourage you to thresh out your own world view to discover any inconsistencies.

Lucy's Children Foundation

I launched *Lucy's Children Foundation* in May 2007 and provided an initial endowment of 100,000 Euros that came from the proceeds of my Lucy book trilogy. Thanks to all of your generous contributions and interest earnings accrued to August 2020, already more than 125,000 Euros could be provided for two deserving charity projects: in the Jhabua-District in central India, a school for impoverished children was built; and since 2013 we've financed night schools in the federal state of Rajasthan for children who can't go to regular schools during the day. The children voluntarily attend school six nights per week from 6-9 PM (in the summer from 7-10 PM). Most of the students are girls. They learn reading, arithmetic, writing, and dealing with everyday situations: Why is clean drinking water so important? How do banks and post offices work? How to care and raise farm animals? The children also receive regular medical care, and they are escorted home after school each night.

Fig. 56: Night school for children in India

Social studies, science, math, Hindi, and English are all taught, and the children's progress is checked every month. Additional courses prepare these children for transition to public schools. One special feature is the establishment of a *children's parliament* which is re-elected every two to three years. This parliament benefits understanding of democracy for the children, and together with a committee of villagers it takes on the important task of carrying out quality control for the school in regular intervals.

Fig. 57: The children's parliament

Lucy's Children Foundation is devoted to investing in loving lives and the education of children: Wholesome food is purchased, sanitary installations and a rainwater tank were built, plenty of teaching materials and even a private school bus for the children were provided. Hundreds of beaming children's eyes say: "Thank you!"

Lucy's Children Foundation

Fig. 58: All donations go directly to the children

I would like to express my heartfelt thanks to Dagmar von Tschurtschenhaler. She is personally responsible for the tremendous success of the night schools in Rajasthan. She visits the children regularly and was kind enough to provide the color pictures. This project has the same aim as my books: build love and understanding in the world without attaching political or religious beliefs. *Lucy's Children Foundation* is recognized by the Revenue Office Munich as a charitable and non-profit organization.

Donation account:	Stiftung Lucys Kinder
IBAN:	DE41 7002 0500 3751 4401 44
Bank:	Bank für Sozialwirtschaft, Munich
BIC:	BFSWDE33MUE

Donations can also be made *online:*
https://www.lucys-kinder.de/?lang=en

Notes

A1 Aurelius M: *Meditations*. Book IV, 40, 121–180ce.

A2 These lines were inspired from the chorus of Ludwig van Beethoven's *Ode to Joy*. Symphony No. 9, Libretto by Friedrich Schiller, 1803 version.

A3 Dunn, JD: *Window of the Soul. The Kabbalah of Rabbi Isaac Luria* (translated by Snyder N). Redwheel Weiser, San Francisco 2008, p. 122. From: *Peri Ez Hayyim*. Hekhal 7, Shaar 48.

1 Filk T, Giolini D: *Am Anfang war die Ewigkeit. Auf der Suche nach dem Ursprung der Zeit*. C. H. Beck, Munich 2004, p. 145.

2 Newton I: *Philosophiae Naturalis Principia Mathematica*. Daniel Adee, New York 1846, p. 77.

3 see note 2.

4 Newton I: *Philosophiae Naturalis Principia Mathematica*. Daniel Adee, New York 1846, p. 78.

5 see note 4.

6 see note 4.

7 Leibniz GW: *Monadologie*, § 32.

8 Alexander RG: *The Leibniz-Clarke Correspondence*. Manchester University Press, Manchester 1998, p. xxxviii.

9 Kant I: *Inaugural Dissertation*. Sect. III, 15, D.

10 Kant I: *Critique of Pure Reason I*. Sect. I, SS 2, 2.

11 see note 10.

12 Kant I: *Critique of Pure Reason I*. Sect. II, SS 5, 2.

13 see note 12.

14 Einstein A: *Zur Elektrodynamik bewegter Körper*. Annalen der Physik 17, 1905, pp. 891–921.

15 "Non-accelerating" means that an object is either at rest or in motion at a constant velocity.

16 see note 14.

17 Einstein A: *Die Grundlage der allgemeinen Relativitätstheorie*. Annalen der Physik 49, 1916, pp. 769–822.

18 Dyson FW, Eddington AS, Davidson C: *A Determination of the Deflection of Light by the Sun's Gravitational Field*. Philosophical Transactions of the Royal Society of London 220, London 1920, pp. 291–333.

19 Hermann A: *Einstein. Eine Biographie*. Piper, Munich 1995, p. 262.

20 Planck Collaboration: *Planck 2015 Results. XIII. Cosmological Parameters*. arXiv Astronomy and Astrophysics, 2016, p. 32.

21 Lemaître G: *Un univers homogène de masse constante et de rayon croissant, rendant compte de la vitesse radiale des nébuleuses extra-galactiques*. Annales de la Société scientifique de Bruxelles 47, Bruxelles 1927, pp. 49–59.

22 Hoyle F: *The Nature of the Universe*. Basil Blackwell, Oxford 1950.

23 Bennett CL et al.: *Cosmic Temperature Fluctuations from Two Years of COBE Differential Microwave Radiometers Observations*. The Astrophysical Journal 436, 1994, pp. 423–442.

24 https://imagine.gsfc.nasa.gov/educators/programs/cosmictimes/educators/guide/age_size.html [31.05.2020]

25 Parmenides: *On Nature*, II–VIII.

26 Parmenides: *On Nature*, III.

27 Heraclitus: *Fragment* 30.

28 Heraclitus: *Fragment* 51.

29 Heraclitus: *Fragment* 91.

30 The Bible: *John* 8:12.

31 Kind DA (editor): *Zeitschrift für Missionskunde und Religionswissenschaft*. Heidelberg 1912, p. 137.

32 Niemz MH: *How Science Can Help Us Live in Peace*. Universal Publishers, Irvine 2018, p. 107.

33 Niemz MH: *How Science Can Help Us Live in Peace*. Universal Publishers, Irvine 2018, p. 81.

34 Niemz MH: *How Science Can Help Us Live in Peace*. Universal Publishers, Irvine 2018, p. 85.

35 As we will see later in this challenge, all light in the universe is actually one big thing.

36 Rilke RM: *Sonette an Orpheus*. 2, XIII.

37 Leibniz GW: *Essais de théodicée sur la bonté de Dieu, la liberté de l'homme et l'origine du mal*. Amsterdam 1710.

38 Steindl-Rast D: *Credo*. Herder, Freiburg 2010, p. 17.

39 The Koran: *Sure* 22:73.

40 Laplace P-S: *A Philosophical Essay on Probabilities* (translated from the original French edition by Truscott FW and Emory FL). Dover Publications, New York 1951, p. 4.

41 Poincaré H: *Sur le problème des trois corps et les équations de la dynamique*. Acta Mathematica 13, 1890, pp. 1–270.

42 It's actually the precise location and precise momentum of a particle that aren't determined at the same time. The *momentum* of a particle is equal to its velocity, but multiplied by its mass.

43 In a letter to Max Born in December 1926, Albert Einstein wrote: "At any rate, I'm convinced that *he* [God] doesn't play dice."

44 Libet B et al.: *Time of Conscious Intention to Act in Relation to Onset of Cerebral Activity (Readiness-Potential). The Unconscious Initiation of a Freely Voluntary Act*. Brain 106, 1983, pp. 623–642.

45 Trevena J, Miller J: *Brain Preparation Before a Voluntary Action: Evidence Against Unconscious Movement Initiation*. Consciousness and Cognition 19, 2010, pp. 447–456.

46 Kornhuber HH, Deecke L: *Hirnpotentialänderungen bei Willkürbewegungen und passiven Bewegungen des Menschen: Bereitschaftspotential und reafferente Potentiale*. Pflüger's Archiv 284, 1965, pp. 1–17.

47 Haggard P, Eimer M: *On the Relation Between Brain Potentials and the Awareness of Voluntary Movements*. Experimental Brain Research 126, 1999, pp. 128–133.

48 Crick F, Koch C: *The Unconscious Homunculus*. Neuropsychoanalysis 2, 2000, pp. 3–11.

49 Tryon EP: *Is the Universe a Vacuum Fluctuation?* Nature 246, 1973, pp. 396–397.

50 Albrecht A, Steinhardt PJ: *Cosmology for Grand Unified Theories with Radiatively Induced Symmetry Breaking*. Physical Review Letters 48, 1982, pp. 1220–1223.

51 Becquerel H: *Sur les radiations émises par phosphorescence*. Comptes Rendus 122, 1896, pp. 420–421.

52 Lazcano A, Miller SL: *The Origin and Early Evolution of Life: Prebiotic Chemistry, the pre-RNA World, and Time*. Cell 85, 1996, pp. 793–798.

53 Dirac PAM: *The Quantum Theory of the Emission and Absorption of Radiation*. Proceedings of the Royal Society 114, 1927, pp. 243–265.

54 https://www.independent.co.uk/news/world/americas/donald-trump-family-separation-us-mexico-border-illegal-immigration-white-house-a8583226.html [31.05.2020]

55 Plutarch: *Moralia*, 636f.

56 Niemz MH: *How Science Can Help Us Live in Peace*. Universal Publishers, Irvine 2018, p. 187.

57 Censorinus: *De Die Natali*, IV, 7.

58 Aristotle: *De Generatione Animalium*.

59 Cuvier G: *Memoir on the Species of Elephants, Both Living and Fossil*. Lecture held at the Muséum National d'Histoire Naturelle, Paris 1796.

60 Cuvier G, Jameson R, Mitchill SL: *Essay on the Theory of the Earth*. Kirk & Mercein, New York 1818, p. 98.

61 Cuvier G: *Le Règne Animal*. Paris 1817.

62 Lamarck J-B: *Recherches sur l'organisation des corps vivants*. Lecture held at the Muséum National d'Histoire Naturelle, Paris 1802.

63 Paley W: *Natural Theology or Evidences of the Existence and Attributes of the Deity*. Philadelphia 1802.

64 Desmond A, Moore JR: *Darwin*. List, Munich 1991, p. 218.

65 Sulloway FJ: *Darwin and His Finches: The Evolution of a Legend*. Journal of the History of Biology 15, 1982, pp. 1–53.

66 The complete title of Charles Darwin's work *On the Origin of Species* is: *On the Origin of Species by Means of Natural Selection*.

67 Lack D: *Darwin's Finches*. Cambridge University Press, Cambridge 1947.

Notes

68   Darwin C: *On the Origin of Species.* John Murray, London 1859.

69   Bredekamp H: *Darwins Korallen. Frühe Evolutionsmodelle und die Tradition der Naturgeschichte.* Wagenbach, Berlin 2005, p. 23.

70   The Bible: *Genesis* 1:28.

71   The Chimpanzee Sequencing and Analysis Consortium: *Initial Sequence of the Chimpanzee Genome and Comparison with the Human Genome.* Nature 437, 2005, pp. 69–87.

72   Crick FH: *The Genetic Code.* Proceedings of the Royal Society of London, Biological Sciences 167, London 1967, pp. 331–347.

73   Clark-Walker GD, Weiller GF: *The Structure of the Small Mitochondrial DNA of Kluyveromyces Thermotolerans Is Likely to Reflect the Ancestral Gene Order in Fungi.* Journal of Molecular Evolution 38, 1994, pp. 593–601.

74   Meyer SC: *Darwin's Doubt. The Explosive Origin of Animal Life and the Case for Intelligent Design.* HarperOne, New York 2014, pp. 353–381.

75   No animal blows itself and other living things to bits "in the name of God."

76   http://www.hindupedia.com/en/Adi_Shankaracharya [31.05.2020]

77   Descartes R: *Die Prinzipien der Philosophie.* Amsterdam 1644, 1, 7.

78   Feuerbach L: *Das Wesen des Christentums.* Leipzig 1841, p. 381.

79   see note 78.

80   Rimbaud A: *Seher-Briefe.* DTV, Munich 1997, p. 367.

81   Hume D: *A Treatise of Human Nature.* 1739, 1.4.6.

82   van Lommel P: *Near-Death Experience, Consciousness, and the Brain.* World Futures 62, 2006, p. 134.

83   Many people consider the strawberry to be a berry because it has a sweet and sour taste and contains a lot of vitamin C. But botanically speaking, the strawberry is not a berry at all, but a so-called *aggregate accessory fruit.* The yellow dots on the strawberry's surface are tiny nuts! The red flesh is only an accessory part.

84   https://en.wikipedia.org/wiki/Major_religious_groups [31.05.2020]

85   McDermott JJ: *Reading the Pentateuch. A Historical Introduction.* Paulist, New York 2002, p. 21.

86 The Bible: *Genesis* 1:1–5.

87 Niemz MH: *How Science Can Help Us Live in Peace.* Universal Publishers, Irvine 2018, p. 199.

88 Hawking S: *A Brief History of Time.* Bantam, New York 1988, p. 141.

89 Hawking S, Mlodinow L: *The Grand Design.* Bantam, New York 2010, p. 108.

90 Larson EJ, Witham L: *Leading Scientists Still Reject God.* Nature 394, 1998, p. 313.

91 Niemz MH: *Sinn.* Kreuz, Freiburg 2013, pp. 85–93.

92 Whitehead AN: *Process and Reality. An Essay in Cosmology.* Free Press, New York 1929.

93 Whitehead AN: *Process and Reality* (corrected edition). Free Press, New York 1979, p. 79.

94 Whitehead AN: *Process and Reality* (corrected edition). Free Press, New York 1979, p. xi.

95 Whitehead AN: *Process and Reality* (corrected edition). Free Press, New York 1979, p. 18.

96 Emmet D: *Creativity and the Passage of Nature.* In: Rapp F, Wiehl R (editors): *Whitehead's Metaphysics of Creativity.* State University of New York Press, New York 1990, p. 63.

97 Whitehead AN: *Process and Reality* (corrected edition). Free Press, New York 1979, p. xiv.

98 Whitehead's *philosophy of organism* is inversely related to Immanuel Kant's *epistemology*. Kant: The world exists from experience that takes place in my head. Whitehead: I exist from the process of experiencing that takes place within the world.

99 Whitehead AN: *Process and Reality* (corrected edition). Free Press, New York 1979, p. 88.

100 Whitehead AN: *Process and Reality* (corrected edition). Free Press, New York 1979, p. 7.

101 see note 100.

102 Whitehead AN: *Process and Reality* (corrected edition). Free Press, New York 1979, p. 22.

103 Whitehead AN: *Process and Reality* (corrected edition). Free Press, New York 1979, pp. 51–52.

104 Whitehead AN: *Process and Reality* (corrected edition). Free Press, New York 1979, p. 34.

105 Whitehead AN: *Process and Reality* (corrected edition). Free Press, New York 1979, p. 185.

106 Whitehead AN: *Process and Reality* (corrected edition). Free Press, New York 1979, pp. 347–348.

107 Jäger W: *Wiederkehr der Mystik*. Herder, Freiburg 2013, p. 11.

108 The Bible: *Exodus* 20:4.

109 see note 30.

110 The Koran: *Sure* 24:35.

111 The Bible: *Psalms* 27:1.

112 *Bhagavad Gita* 13:17.

113 see note 31.

114 The Bible: *Galatians* 5:14.

115 Niemz MH: *How Science Can Help Us Live in Peace*. Universal Publishers, Irvine 2018, pp. 19–37.

116 Greene B: *The Fabric of the Cosmos*. Vintage, New York 2005, p. 266.

117 Aristoteles: *Metaphysics* VII, 17, 1041b.

118 https://www.genome.gov/human-genome-project/Completion-FAQ [31.05.2020]

119 Dawkins R: *The Blind Watchmaker*. Penguin, London 2006, p. 43.

120 Dawkins R: *The Blind Watchmaker*. Penguin, London 2006, p. 49.

121 Schröder K-P, Smith RC: *Distant Future of the Sun and Earth Revisited*. Monthly Notices of the Royal Astronomical Society 386, 2008, pp. 155–163.

122 Dawkins R: *The Blind Watchmaker*. Penguin, London 2006, p. 5.

123 Here is the success recipe for a happy partnership between two people: Always value higher those things that you can do together than what either one of you can do alone!

124 Moody RA: *Life After Life.* HarperOne, New York 2015, pp. 51–57.

125 Since there is no plural for "consciousness," it must be an all-embracing cosmic consciousness.

126 Dalai Lama, Alt F: *Der Appell des Dalai Lama an die Welt.* Benevento Publishing, Salzburg 2016, p. 6.

127 see note 115.

128 Dalai Lama, Alt F: *Der Appell des Dalai Lama an die Welt.* Benevento Publishing, Salzburg 2016, p. 36.

129 Lutz A, Greischar LL, Rawlings NB, Ricard M, Davidson RJ: *Long-Term Meditators Self-Induce High-Amplitude Gamma Synchrony During Mental Practice.* Proceedings of the National Academy of Sciences 101, 2004, pp. 16369–16373.

130 A spacecraft with such velocity isn't technically possible today, but this does not affect the relativity of spatial and temporal distances in any way.

131 Niemz MH: *Bin ich, wenn ich nicht mehr bin?* Kreuz, Freiburg 2011, p. 69.

132 see note 131.

133 Ring K: *Life at Death.* Coward, McCann and Geoghegan, New York 1980, chap. 3.

134 Ruder H, Nollert HP: *Einsteins Holodeck.* Spektrum der Wissenschaft 7, 2005, pp. 56–65.

135 The details of this flight are described in: Nollert HP, Ruder H: *Die relativistische Welt in Bildern. Was Einstein gerne gesehen hätte.* Spektrum der Wissenschaft Spezial 3, 2005.

136 Niemz MH: *Lucy mit c.* BoD, Norderstedt 2008, p. 36.

137 Niemz MH: *How Science Can Help Us Live in Peace.* Universal Publishers, Irvine 2018, p. 104.

138 Ring K, Elsaesser-Valarino E: *Im Angesicht des Lichts.* Ariston, Kreuzlingen 1999, pp. 28–29.

139 Moody RA: *Life After Life.* HarperOne, New York 2015, pp. 57–67.

140 Obama B: From his *Commencement Address* given at the University of Massachusetts, Boston, 02 June 2006.

Picture Credits

Copyright if not specified otherwise: © Markolf H. Niemz

Fig. 13: https://commons.wikimedia.org/wiki/File:Cobe-cosmic-background-radiation.gif [31.05.2020]

Fig. 14 (b/w photograph of Abraham Lincoln): https://commons.wikimedia.org/wiki/File:Abraham_Lincoln_head_on_shoulders_photo_portrait.jpg [31.05.2020]

Fig. 14 (color photograph of Abraham Lincoln): https://mymodernmet.com/kazuhiro-tsuji-portrait-of-lincoln/ [31.05.2020]

Fig. 25: https://commons.wikimedia.org/wiki/File:Darwin%27s_finches_by_Gould.jpg [31.05.2020]

Fig. 27: https://commons.wikimedia.org/wiki/File:Darwin_tree.png [31.05.2020]

Fig. 31 left: https://commons.wikimedia.org/wiki/File:Romanesco_Broccoli_detail_-_(1).jpg [31.05.2020]

Fig. 31 right: https://commons.wikimedia.org/wiki/File:Mandel_zoom_14_satellite_julia_island.jpg [31.05.2020]

Fig. 34 left: https://www.its.caltech.edu/~atomic/snowcrystals/class/w050207a039.jpg [31.05.2020] © Kenneth G. Libbrecht

Fig. 34 center: Mosquito eye, by Raija Peura, University of Oulu, Institute of Electron Optics' Image Gallery

Fig. 35 center: https://en.wikipedia.org/wiki/File:Arianta_arbustorum_-_Braunau-1968.jpg [31.05.2020] © Tom Meijer

Fig. 35 right: https://de.wikipedia.org/wiki/Datei:Ssc2003-06c.jpg [31.05.2020]

Fig. 39 left: https://commons.wikimedia.org/wiki/File:Wet_Lorikeet.jpg [31.05.2020] © Louise Docker

Figs. 52a-c: With kind permission of H.-P. Nollert and H. Ruder, Institute of Theoretical Astrophysics, University of Tuebingen, Germany

Figs. 53a-c: With kind permission of H.-P. Nollert and H. Ruder, Institute of Theoretical Astrophysics, University of Tuebingen, Germany

Figs. 54-58: With kind permission of D. von Tschurtschenthaler

Page 21: https://commons.wikimedia.org/wiki/File:GodfreyKneller-IsaacNewton-1689.jpg [31.05.2020]

Picture Credits

Page 23: https://commons.wikimedia.org/wiki/File:Samuel_Clarke_NPG_extract.jpg [31.05.2020]

Page 25: https://commons.wikimedia.org/wiki/File:Kant_foto.jpg [31.05.2020]

Page 32: https://commons.wikimedia.org/wiki/File:Albert_Einstein_1921_by_F_Schmutzer.jpg [31.05.2020]

Page 40 (color photograph of Abraham Lincoln): https://mymodernmet.com/kazuhiro-tsuji-portrait-of-lincoln/ [31.05.2020]

Page 43: https://commons.wikimedia.org/wiki/Category:Parmenides_of_Elea#/media/File:Parmenides.jpg [31.05.2020]

Page 46: https://commons.wikimedia.org/wiki/File:Heraclitus,_Johannes_Moreelse.jpg [31.05.2020]

Page 59: https://commons.wikimedia.org/wiki/File:Andromeda_Galaxy_(with_h-alpha).jpg [31.05.2020] © Adam Evans

Page 68: https://commons.wikimedia.org/wiki/File:Christoph_Bernhard_Francke_-_Bildnis_des_Philosophen_Leibniz_(ca._1695).jpg [31.05.2020]

Page 71: https://commons.wikimedia.org/wiki/File:Pierre-Simon_Laplace.jpg [31.05.2020]

Page 92: https://commons.wikimedia.org/wiki/File:Georges_Cuvier_large.jpg [31.05.2020]

Page 93: https://commons.wikimedia.org/wiki/File:Jean-Baptiste_de_Lamarck.jpg [31.05.2020]

Page 95: https://commons.wikimedia.org/wiki/File:Charles_Darwin_by_G._Richmond.jpg [31.05.2020]

Page 107: https://commons.wikimedia.org/wiki/File:Bundesarchiv_Bild183-R57262,_Werner_Heisenberg.jpg [31.05.2020]

Page 115: https://commons.wikimedia.org/wiki/File:%27Moses%27_by_Michelangelo_JBU160.jpg [31.05.2020]

Page 118: https://de.m.wikipedia.org/wiki/Datei:Physicist_Stephen_Hawking_in_Zero_Gravity_NASA.jpg [31.05.2020]

Page 120: https://commons.wikimedia.org/wiki/File:Alfred_North_Whitehead_-_cropped.jpg [31.05.2020]

Page 176: Markolf H. Niemz © Torsten Zimmermann

Page 184: With kind permission of D. von Tschurtschenthaler

Contact the Author

Professor Markolf H. Niemz is pleased to give readings and lectures throughout Europe, the USA, and Canada. You will find all events on his official website:

http://www.markolfniemz.de/en

If you wish to invite the author to a reading or if you wish to support his work, you are welcome to contact him here:

markolf.niemz@lucys-kinder.de

Markolf H. Niemz is a full professor of biomedical engineering at Heidelberg University, Germany, founded in 1386. He has a PhD in physics and a MSc in bioengineering from the University of California at San Diego. Niemz was a research fellow at the Wellman Labs, Harvard Medical School. In 1995, he was awarded the Karl-Freudenberg-Prize by the Heidelberg Academy of Sciences. Niemz is the author of many European bestsellers on modern science and spirituality. His lucid readings and lectures always attract a great audience.

www.ingramcontent.com/pod-product-compliance
Lightning Source LLC
Chambersburg PA
CBHW051054160426
43193CB00010B/1181